CHILTON'S Repair and Tune-Up Guide

Volvo

1956–69

ILLUSTRATED

Prepared by the

Automotive Editorial Department

CHILTON BOOK COMPANY
RADNOR, PENNSYLVANIA

Chilton Way, Radnor, Pa. 19089
Published in Radnor, Pa., by Chilton Book Company
and simultaneously in Ontario, Canada,
by Thomas Nelson & Sons, Ltd.

ISBN 0-8019-5635-8
ISBN 0-8019-6529-2 pbk.
Library of Congress Catalog Card No. 73-146881
Manufactured in the United States of America
567890 09

ACKNOWLEDGMENTS

Chilton Book Company expresses appreciation to these firms for their generous assistance:

ROBERT BOSCH CORPORATION
Long Island City, New York

CHAMPION SPARK PLUG COMPANY
Toledo, Ohio

THE GOODYEAR TIRE & RUBBER COMPANY
Akron, Ohio

Contents

Chapter 1
Identification and Maintenance

The Volvo Story

The world's first production Volvo—an open touring car with a 28-bhp, four-cylinder engine—rolled off the assembly line in Gothenburg, April 14, 1927, heralding the beginning of the Swedish car company Aktiebolaget Volvo and climaxing the dreams of businessman Assar Gabrielsson and technician Gustaf Larsson.

It was only three years earlier that Gabrielsson and Larsson had set out to start a car company, but it must have seemed to them a lifetime. In 1924, there was a pall of depression on the market. The motor industry was entirely dominated by imported cars. Most observers prophesied quick failure for the Swedish car company, and nobody was willing to risk investing in the adventurous project. However, Gabrielsson and Larsson saw several factors favoring a car industry in Sweden. And so, to impress certain financiers, the two pioneers completed drawings for their future car and began manufacture with their own capital. Their system of assembling cars—building some parts and procuring others from subsuppliers (a few of whom now constitute the core of the AB Volvo Manufacturing Group)—gave rise to the expression, "building cars the Volvo way," which has followed Volvo through the years.

Gabrielsson and Larsson completed ten test vehicles, and the following year, in 1926, their efforts were rewarded: a far-sighted group—directors of the Swedish Ball Bearing Company (SKF)—invested large capital in the newly established company. They named it Volvo (Latin for "I roll") after a subsidiary of SKF. Within months, Volvo cars were being exported to several Scandinavian countries. But Volvo did not enter the U.S. market until 1956.

Early Volvos set the basic design for years to come. Then in 1944, a revolutionary car which had been designed during the war was introduced. This model, the PV 444/544 became one of Volvo's outstanding successes, paralleled only by the 1957 model 121/122S cars that have long topped Swedish registration statistics and dominated many of the export markets. The 122S in the U.S. in 1966 became the third best selling import sedan, demand

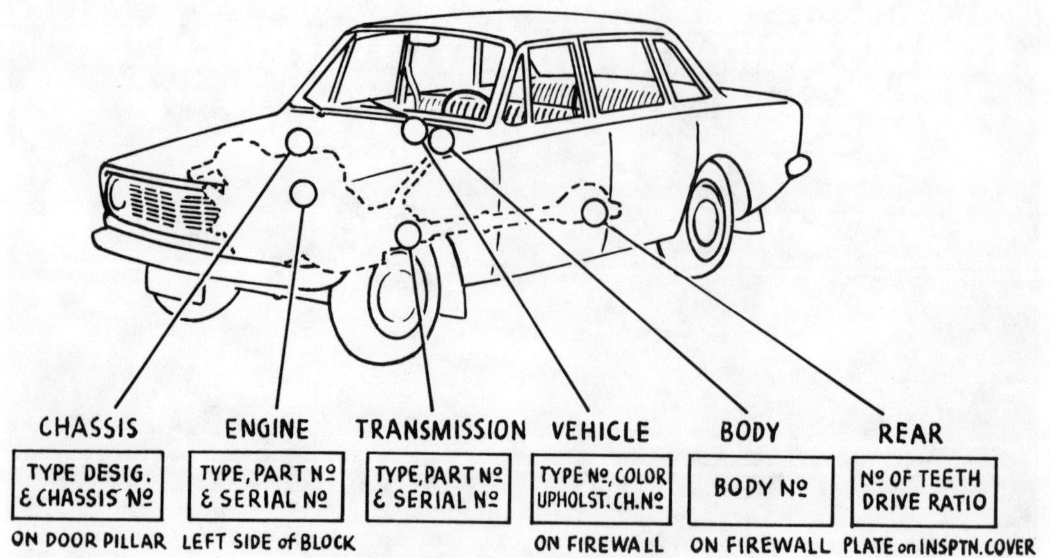

Series 144 vehicle identification.

exceeding the supply despite a price competitive to U.S. cars. The 122S is a two-door sedan with a 100 hp, twin-carb, 4-cylinder engine of 109 cubic inches.

Volvo's excellent materials and workmanship were never more manifest than in the Model 1800S GT sport coupe introduced in 1964. Also a 109 cubic inch engine, the 1800S offers good handling and a top speed of 110 mph. A five main bearing crankshaft is one of many extra design features. Clutch pedal pressure is reduced by a diaphragm type pressure spring rather than the usual coil springs.

In 1967, Volvo added a luxury, contemporary style four-door compact known as the 144S (two-door, 142S) with all the safety devices pioneered by Volvo over many years, such as padded interiors, disc brakes, collapsible steering wheel, shoulder lap seat belts, and doors that stay closed on impact. Volvo was first to offer shoulder lap seat belts, and they are standard equipment on these cars.

In 1968 the 140 line was supplemented with the addition of a station wagon, the Model 145S. More modern than the 122S station wagon, it includes all the luxuries and safety items of the 140 series. At the time of the introduction of the 145S, the B18 engine was replaced with the two liter B20 engine.

In 1969, the Volvo line was again expanded by the introduction of the luxurious, powerful Model 164. This prestigious automobile is powered by a three liter, six cylinder engine. The B30 engine is a direct descendant of the thoroughly reliable B20 engine.

With 17 factories throughout the country, Volvo is Sweden's largest individual exporter. It is the second largest engineering concern in Scandinavia, exporting high quality products worldwide to more than 130 different markets.

How To Take Care of Your Volvo

Tools

This book contains the recommended Volvo tool number where applicable. It is not necessary to use only the Volvo tool, as many of the tools are fairly standard in any garage. For specialized service tools, see your Volvo dealer.

Model Identification

In all correspondence with the dealer or when ordering spare parts, the type designation, chassis number and engine number of the Volvo should be quoted for proper identification.

Type designation and chassis number are stamped on the cowl under the hood (on the right door column in the 144S and 164S). The type designation is also stamped on a plate to the left of this, with the code number for body color and upholstery. The engine type designation, part number and serial number are given on the left side of the cylinder block. Stamped on a tab are the last figures of the part number followed by the serial number. In identifying the engine, both the part number and serial number should be given.

Recommended Lubrication

Getting continuous top performance from fine machinery requires periodic maintenance using recommended lubricants.

Engine oil level is accurately shown on the dip stick only when the engine is warm but *not* running preferably after sitting awhile to allow oil to drain into sump.

When flushing crankcase appears advisable, use the proper quantity of 10W oil (See table) and idle engine at 1000 rpm until oil is hot. Drain crankcase and filter immediately after stopping engine. Install new filter and recommended oil.

Engine Identification

Number of Cylinders	*Displacement Cu. In. (cc)*	*Type*	*Model*
4	86(1410)	OHV	B-14A
4	96.4(1580)	OHV	B-16A
4	96.4(1580)	OHV	B-16B
4	96.4(1580)	OHV	B-16D
4	109(1780)	OHV	B-18A
4	109(1780)	OHV	B-18B
4	109(1780)	OHV	B-18D
4	122(1990)	OHV	B-20A
4	122(1990)	OHV	B-20B
6	183(2980)	OHV	B-30A

Replacing oil filter every 6,000 miles requires care when tightening retaining nut. One-half turn beyond firm contact should adequately seal the gasket. Check for leaks after starting engine.

Vehicle Identification

Year	*Model*		*Starting Chassis Number*
1956	PV444		-
1957	PV444		-
1958	PV444		151123
1959	PV444		18501
1959	PV544		196005
1960	PV544		240387
1961	PV544		244000
1962	PV544/C		302360/ 330100
1963	PV544		334061
1964	PV544		369000
1965	PV544		406043
1966	PV544		427078
1959	122		21000
1960			28167
1961			29000
1962		122	55741
1963	(4 door)	122	87743
1963	(2 door)	122	2461
1964	(4 door)	122	112000
1964	(2 door)	122	11600
1965	(4 door)	122	150532
1965	(2 door)	122	57555
1966	(4 door–stick)	122	176814
1966	(4 door–automatic)	122	176822
1966	(2 door–stick)	122	108243
1966	(2 door–automatic)	122	108258
1966	(Station Wagon)	122	22217
1962	P1800		101
1963	P1800		326
1964	1800S		6001
1965	1800S		9247
1966	1800S		13679
1967	1800S		-
1968	1800S		-
1969	1800		-
1970	1800		-
1967	142		-
1968	142		-
1969	142		-
1970	142		-
1967	144		-
1968	144		-
1969	144		-
1970	144		-
1968	145		-
1969	145		-
1970	145		-
1969	164		-
1970	164		-

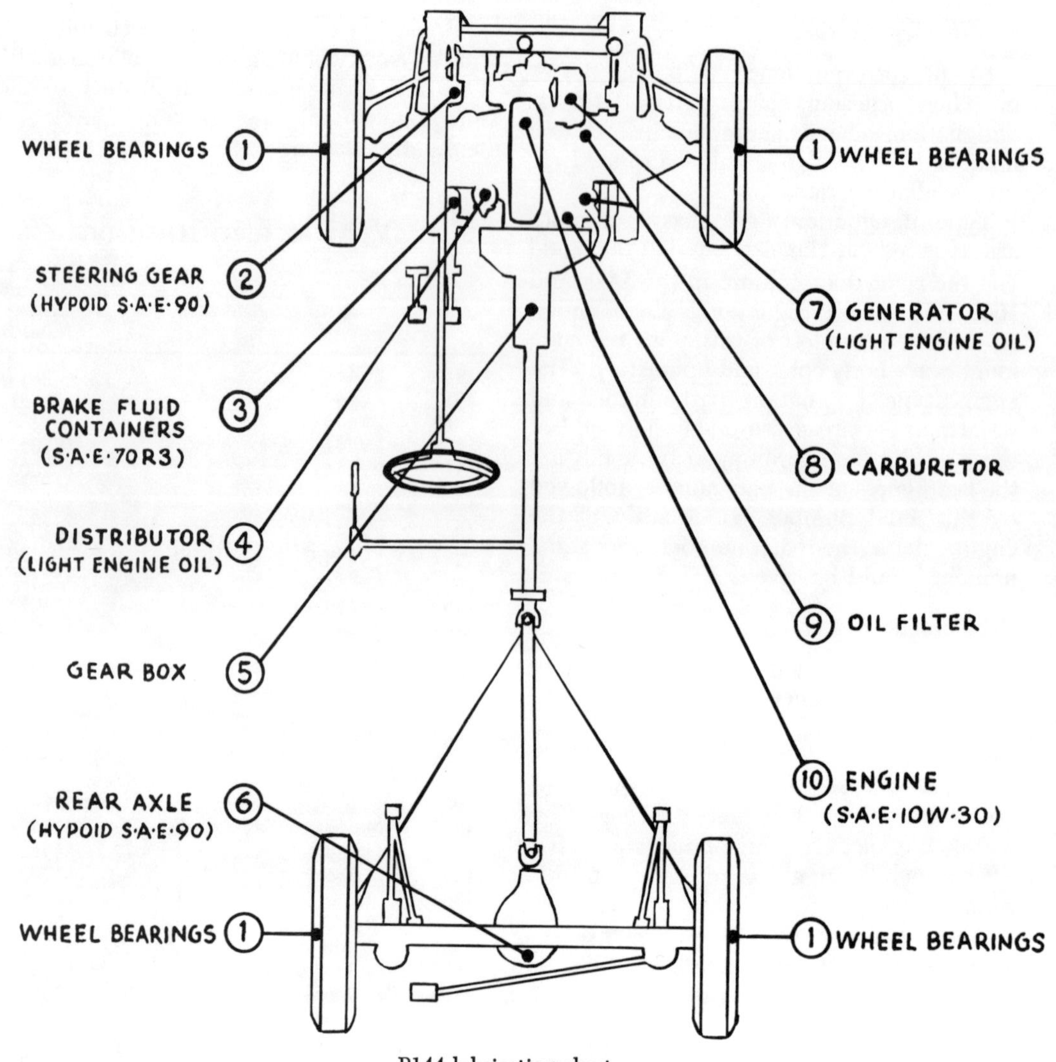

P144 lubricating chart.

1. The wheel bearings are filled at the factory with a special type grease which covers the entire lifetime of the bearing. For this reason, it is not necessary to change or add lubricant. This also applies after reconditioning or changing of the bearings, provided that the bearings are then lubricated with a high-class grease.
2. Check that oil reaches up to the filler plug. Use hypoid oil SAE 80 all year round.
3. Check that the brake fluid reaches up to the Max mark. If necessary, add brake fluid which meets the requirements according to SAE 70 R 3.
4. Use light engine oil in the distributor.
5. Every 300 miles, check that the oil reaches up to the filler plug. Change oil after every 25,000 miles. Note: The quality of oil needed depends on the type of gearbox.
6. Every 3000 miles, check that the oil reaches up to the filler plug. Use hypoid SAE 90.
7. Fill the lubricating cap, if fitted, with light engine oil. The lubricating cap is opened by turning the outer cap. Use an ordinary can, not a force-feed type.
8. Check the oil level in the carburetor when changing the engine oil.
9. Change the oil filter every 6000 miles.
10. Check the oil level every time you buy gas.

Using oil of proper viscosity aids cold starting by increasing cranking speed.

Change transmission oil by removing drain plug at bottom of housing. Wipe area clean and remove filter plug. Fill overdrive transmissions with SAE 30 lubricant so that oil comes up to fill plug opening when car is level. Capacity is 3½ pints; 3 pints for the 164. Fill standard transmissions with SAE 90. Capacity 1½ pints. Capacity of automatic transmissions is 13¼ pints of Type A lubricant.

No lubrication fittings are provided on Volvos except on the clutch controls of B16 engines. All bearings and joints are either sealed and self lubricating or use materials not requiring lubrication.

Engine Oil

Temperature Ranges	*Viscosity*
Above 90°F.	30W, SAE 10W-30
Above Freezing (+32° to 90°F.)	20W, SAE 10W-30
Between 0° and +32°F.	10W, SAE 10W-30
Below 0°F.*	5W, SAE 5W-20

* SAE 5W oil is not recommended for sustained high speed driving. SAE 5W-30 can also be used in this temperature range.

Note: When changing the oil during the Autumn and Winter seasons, consider the lowest anticipated temperature for the next 60 days.

Rear axle requires SAE 90 multipurpose gear lubricant. Capacity is 2.75 pints; 3⅓ for the 164.

Steering system oil ordinarily need not be changed. However, when the level is low, fill with SAE 90 lubricant. Capacity is ½ pint; 1⅓ for the 164.

Lubricate carburetor linkage at all pivot points with one or two drops of engine oil while moving throttle controls. Oil accelerator pump rods. Disconnect all ball joints, fill cups with high temperature grease or lubriplate and reconnect. Move linkage back and forth to check for proper functioning.

Check oil level in SU carburetor damping cylinders at every lubrication. Do not overfill. Use SAE 20 (not SAE 10-30) or automatic transmission fluid.

Lubricate distributor cam with non-corrosive high temperature grease. Remove distributor cap, lift off the rotor and apply a thin coating to the cam. Do not allow grease or dirt to contaminate breaker points.

Hinges and locks of luggage compartment and doors should be lubricated every 6,000 miles or at least once a year to avoid squeaks and eliminate unnecessary wear. Use stick type graphite lubricant on door jamb strikers. Take an additional few minutes to clear door and body drain holes so that water cannot be trapped. In freezing weather, door and luggage compartment locks should be treated with a suitable lubricant to prevent them from freezing.

Maintenance Suggestions

The Appendix presents units of the metric system with the English equivalents, matching the precision of each to the nearest 1/100,000 .

However, the mechanic who becomes familiar with the metric system won't be troubled with looking up conversions to factory-issued metric specifications. Common metric sizes are not the common American sizes—finding American wrenches to fit an uncommon size is frequently difficult. The best preparation for working on any imported engine is to master the metric system and use a set of metric tools.

Because British terminology for European assemblies and components is most

Frequent Maintenance Checks

Engine Oil	Check level. Change every 6000 miles or 2 months with multi-grade oil, every 3000 miles or 2 months with single grade oil.
Battery Fluid	Check level. Add chemical-free drinking water. Do not over-fill; neutralize spilled acid with baking soda and flush with clean water.
Engine Coolant	Check level. Note presence of sediment. Refill drained radiator with anti-freeze solution.
Lubrication	Hinges and locks; windshield wiper linkage; carburetor linkage.
Tires	Check pressure and wear.

6000-Mile Inspection and Maintenance

General	
Leaks	Visual check for fuel, oil.
Fluid Levels	Transmission, rear axle, master brake cylinder.
Filters	Clean fuel pump strainers, sediment bowl, oil-damp air cleaner. Replace air filter cartridge, oil filter.
Lubrication	Wheel bearings, suspension parts, carburetor linkage, chassis fittings.
Electrical	
Battery	Check condition of charge, clean cables.
Ignition	
Spark Plugs	Inspect, clean or replace, set electrode gap.
Distributor	Lubricate cam, inspect and clean or replace points, reset.
Timing	Check timing and reset if necessary.
Carburetor	
Fuel Flow	Check for proper jetting and atomization of fuel.
Idle Speed	Set idle speed.
Engine	
Valve Clearance	Check against specifications and reset if necessary.
Crankcase	Inspect Positive Crankcase Ventilation valve.
Fan Belt	Inspect belt and correct the tension if necessary.
Compression	Test for equal compression in all cylinders.
Rocker Arm Shaft	Check tighteners.
Clutch	
	Check pedal travel and free play.
Suspension	
Control Arm Ball Joints	Check for wear.
Front Axle	Check for excessive play.
Wheels	
Alignment	Tighten wheel nuts, correct balance, adjust alignment.
Brakes	Test for proper operation, fluid leaks, adequate pedal.
Pads and linings	Remove wheel and inspect. Measure wear.
Tires	
	Rotate and check pressure.

often used in translations from German, it is advantageous to understand the British wording. If communication with European manufacturers ever becomes necessary, writing the British phraseology will prevent confusion and wrong deliveries. Some terms are given in the text in parentheses, and a more complete listing of British terms and American equivalents is in the Appendix.

Battery Care

Volvos with B18 engines have used 12-volt batteries since 1962. Earlier B14 and B16 models were equipped with 6-volt systems. The Volvo 12-volt electrical system requires that the battery produce at least 9 volts while starter is cranking the engine. The 6-volt system can tolerate a minimum of 4.5 volts output under the cranking load.

Batteries should be checked periodically for proper output and good connections. A weak power supply lowers the efficiency of the engine and places a greater drag on the generator circuit.

Inspect the battery case for cracks and weakness. A leaky battery should be replaced. Check the density (specific gravity) of the battery electrolyte with a hydrometer. Readings from a fully charged battery will depend on the make but will fall in the range of 1.260 to 1.310 times as heavy as pure water at 80°F. NOTE: *all cells should produce nearly equal readings.* If one or two cell readings are sharply lower, the cells are defective, and if readings continue to be low after charging, the battery must be replaced. (See Battery Replacement—Chapter 5).

As a battery releases its charge, sulphate ions in the electrolyte become attached to the battery plates—reducing the density of the fluid. The specific gravity of the electrolyte varies not only with the percentage of acid in the liquid, but also with temperature. As temperature increases, the electrolyte expands so that specific gravity is reduced in this second way. As temperature drops, the electrolyte contracts and gravity increases. To correct readings for temperature variations, add .004 to the hydrometer reading for every 10°F. that the electrolyte is above 80°F. and subtract .004 for every 10°F. that the electrolyte is below 80°F. The drawing shows the total correction to make for any temperature above or below 80°F.

The amount of charge remaining in a battery can be roughly determined from the specific gravity ranges shown in the chart below.

Hydrometer Readings	*Condition*
1.260–1.310	Fully charged
1.230–1.250	¾ charged
1.200–1.220	½ charged
1.170–1.190	¼ charged
1.140–1.160	Almost discharged
1.110–1.130	Fully discharged

Perform a light-load voltage test to detect weak cells. First draw off the transient (surface) charge by operating the starter for three seconds and then turning on the low beam lights. After one minute, test each cell (with lights still on) with a voltmeter. A fully charged battery will have no cell voltage below 1.95 volts and no cell should vary more than .05 volts from the others. A greater variation at full charge indicates a defective cell.

Another battery check involves connecting a charger for three minutes under 40 amperes for a 12-volt battery (75 amps for 6-v). Read the battery voltage with the charger still operating. Voltage over 15.5 v for 12-volt battery (7.75 for 6 v) indicates a defective battery. If battery voltage is under this limit and individual cell readings are within 0.1 volts the battery is usable.

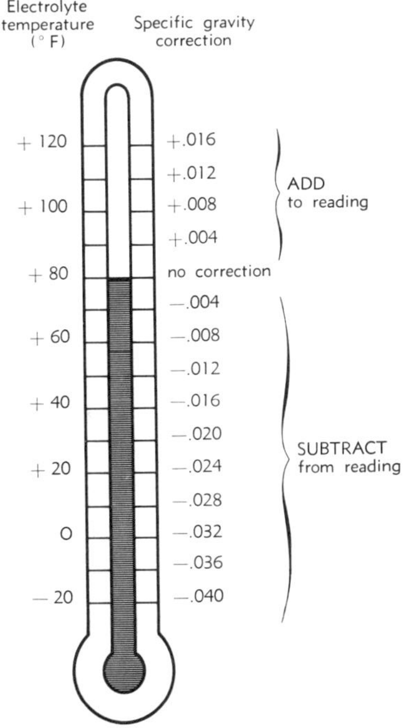

Temperature affects the specific gravity readings of batteries.

Charging a weak battery is best done by a slow-charge method. If quick charging is attempted, check the cell voltages and the color of the electrolyte a few minutes after charge is started. If cell voltages are not uniform or if electrolyte is discolored with brown sediment, quick charging should be stopped in favor of a slow charge. In either case, do not let electrolyte temperature exceed 120°F.

If high electrical circuit voltage is suspected, the voltage regulator might be cutting in abnormally due to corroded or loose battery connections. The symptoms are hard starting, full ammeter charge and lights flaring brightly. After cleaning, coat battery terminals with petroleum jelly (vaseline) to prevent recurrence of problem.

Overcharging the battery is a common cause of battery failure. A symptom of overcharging is a frequent need for addition of water to the battery. The generating system should be corrected immediately to prevent internal battery damage.

Cooling System

The engine is cooled by a pressurized system with a capacity of 9 quarts for the four cylinder engines and 13 quarts for the six. A double acting thermostat, with an opening temperature of 169°F. for the B18 and 179°F. for the B20 and B30, speeds up heating of the engine and assures optimum temperature under all operating conditions. The coolant level should be checked at each refueling.

Replace radiator coolant once a year, when the entire cooling system should be flushed clean with water. The recommended coolant is a mixture consisting of 40% ethylene glycol (Volvo Part No. 297176) and 60% water. To drain the cooling system, open the drain cock on the engine and remove the plug at the bottom of the radiator. Remove the expansion tank and empty its contents into the radiator.

Capacities and Pressures

	Crankcase		*Transmission*		*Rear Axle*		*Fuel*		*Cooling System*	
Engine Model	*Capacity w/o filter (with filter) Pints*	*Viscosity SAE*	*Cap. Pints*	*Vis-cosity SAE*	*Cap. Pints*	*Vis-cosity SAE*	*Tank Cap. Gals.*	*Fuel Pump Press. PSI*	*Cap. with Heater Qts.*	*Therm. Opens °F.*
B14	7 (7.75)	10W-30					9.3	2 to 3		
B16A	6 (7)	10W-30					9.3	2 to 3.5	9.5	
B16B	6 (7)	10W-30	2	90	2		9.3	2 to 3.5	9	169
B18A	7 (8)	10W-30	1.5	90	2.75	90	11.8	1.5 to 3.5	9	169
B18B	7 (8)	10W-30	1.5	90	2.75	90	11.8	1.5 to 3.5	9	169
B18D	7 (8)	10W-30	1.5	90	2.75	90		1.5 to 3.5	9	169
B20	7 (8)	10W-30	1.6	90	2.75	90		1.5 to 3.5	9	169
B30	11 (12.7)	10W-30	1.3	90	3.4	90		2.1 to 3.5	13	179

Notes: **1. Overdrive transmission requires 3.4 pints SAE 30.**
2. Automatic transmissions require 13.25 pints type A oil.

When refilling, the heater control must be set at "Max" heat so that the entire system can be filled. Fill the radiator to the top and put on the cap. Then fill the expansion tank to the "Max" mark or just above. Warm the engine and then check to make sure that the radiator is completely full and that the level lies between the marks on the expansion tank.

Effective cooling system protection against rust requires at least a 25% solution of the recommended antifreeze (+10°F.) through summer and winter. If water only is used, a water pump lubricant and a heavy duty cooling system protector should be added. Methanol or alcohol alone are not recommended for the Volvo cooling system. These agents with their low boiling points evaporate (boil off) in a short time. Ethylene glycol antifreeze compounds have boiling points close to 400°F., well above the heat range of water cooled engines. Anti-rust and lubrication additives are helpful in lubricating the water pump and protecting metal parts. The rust and foam inhibitors used in antifreeze lose their power with aging, particularly in older engines, with greater rust deposits. Antifreeze, itself, eventually loses its protective properties and becomes an irritant to the cooling system. Replace at the recommended intervals.

Antifreeze is harmful to the oil system of the engine. If cooling system fluid has leaked into the engine oil, ethylene-glycol-monobutyl-cellusolve, available from jobbers, is recommended for flushing the system.

Water condensation in the engine is often caused by limited use of the car. If an engine runs only two or three miles before being shut down, it does not maintain its proper operating temperature long enough to evaporate water that may be present in the crankcase. Regular oil changes will help eliminate water accumulation. Also check the thermostat for too-quick opening. If necessary, change the thermostat for hotter engine operation.

Fan Belt Adjustment

A tight fan belt will cause rapid wear of the generator and water pump bearings. A loose fan belt will slip and wear excessively, causing noise, engine overheating and fluctuating generator output. Fan belt tension is correct when light finger pressure deflects the belt one-half inch, or when a pull of 17 to 24 lbs. (8-11 kg) is required to slide the pulley. To measure this, pull the fan in the direction of engine rotation with a spring balance attached to one of the four blades at a point six inches out from the fan hub. An oily or frayed fan belt should be re-

Clutch Specifications

	B16 Engine in. (mm)	*B18 Engine in. (mm)*	*B20 Engine in. (mm)*	*B30 Engine in. (mm)*
Clutch Pedal Free Travel	.37"–.59" (10–15)	.37"–.59" (10–15)	.37"–.59" (10–15)	.37"–.59" (10–15)
Clutch Yoke Free Travel	.12" (3)	.12" (3)	.12" (3)	.12" (3)
Type	Single dry plate disc	Single dry plate disc	Single dry plate disc	Single dry plate disc
Size	8" (203)	8.5" (215.9)	8.5" (215.9)	9"
Pedal-Actuated Control	Mechanical	Hydraulic	Mechanical ①	Mechanical ①
Total Friction Area	52.7 sq. in. $(340)^2$	68 sq. in. $(440)^2$	68.2 sq. in. $(440)^2$	72.5 sq. in. $(468)^2$
Installed Plate Thickness	.28"–.29" (7–7.5)	.28"–.29" (7–7.5)		
Number and Size of Rivets	16; .14" x .25" (3.5 x 6.5)	16; .14" x .21" (3.5 x 5.5)	16; .14" x .21" (3.5 x 5.5)	
Number of Springs; length, loaded under 188–199 lb. (85.5–90.5 kg)	6; 1.5" (38)	6; 1.5" (38)		
Distance between Flywheel and Contact Surface of Clutch Levers with Throw-out Bearing	1.81" (46)	1.81" (46)		
① **Right-hand steering and 1800S - hydraulic control.**	Adjustment of Clutch Levers:	Alternative 1: .29" (7.5) below adjusting jig hub (SVO2065) within ±.06" (1.5) and within .01" (.25) of each other.	Adjustment 41.5" in clutch fixture SVO2322 with packing blocks No. O.	Alternative 2: Adjustment 40.5" in clutch fixture SVO2322 with packing blocks No. O.

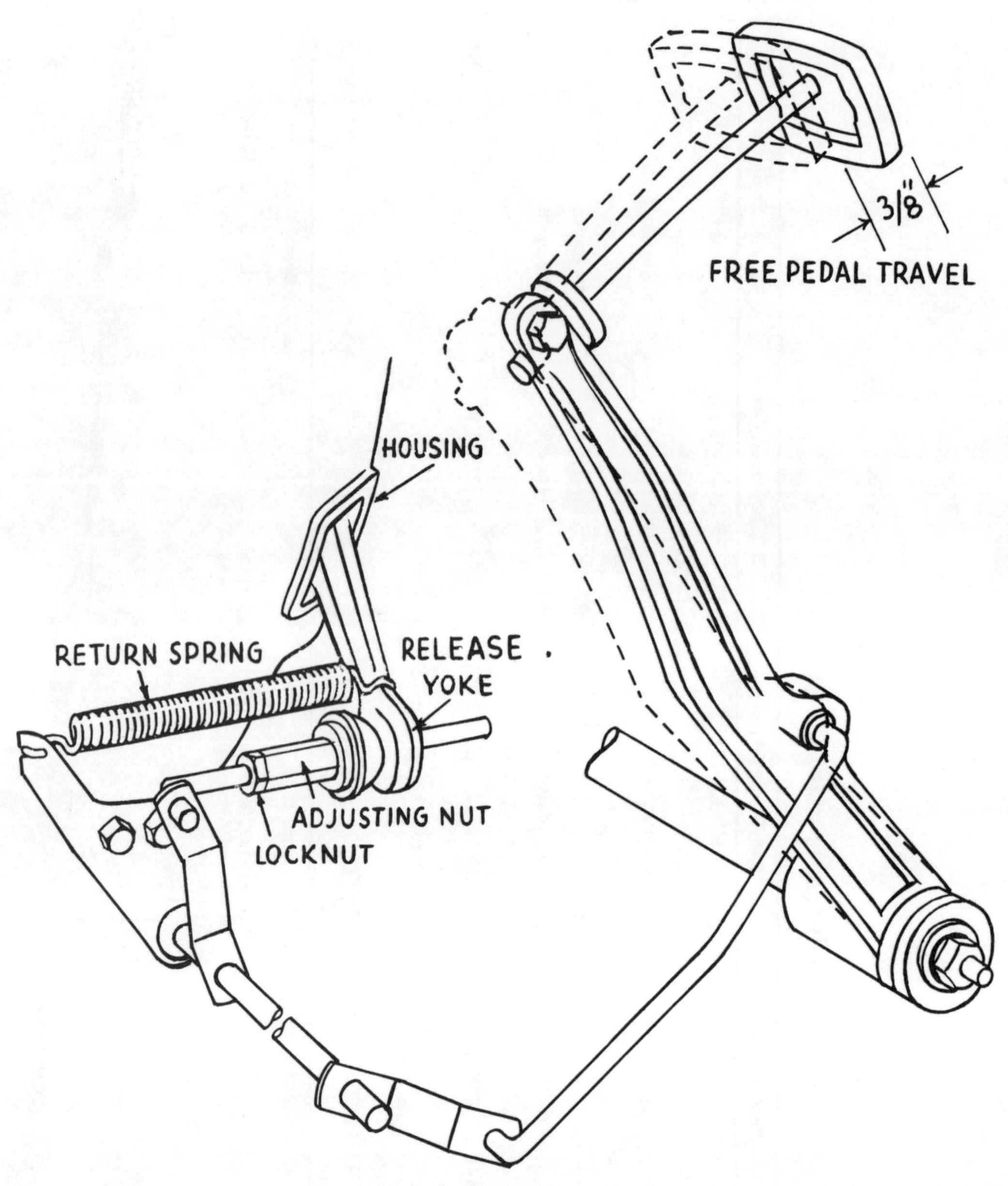

Clutch adjustment, PV544, P210.

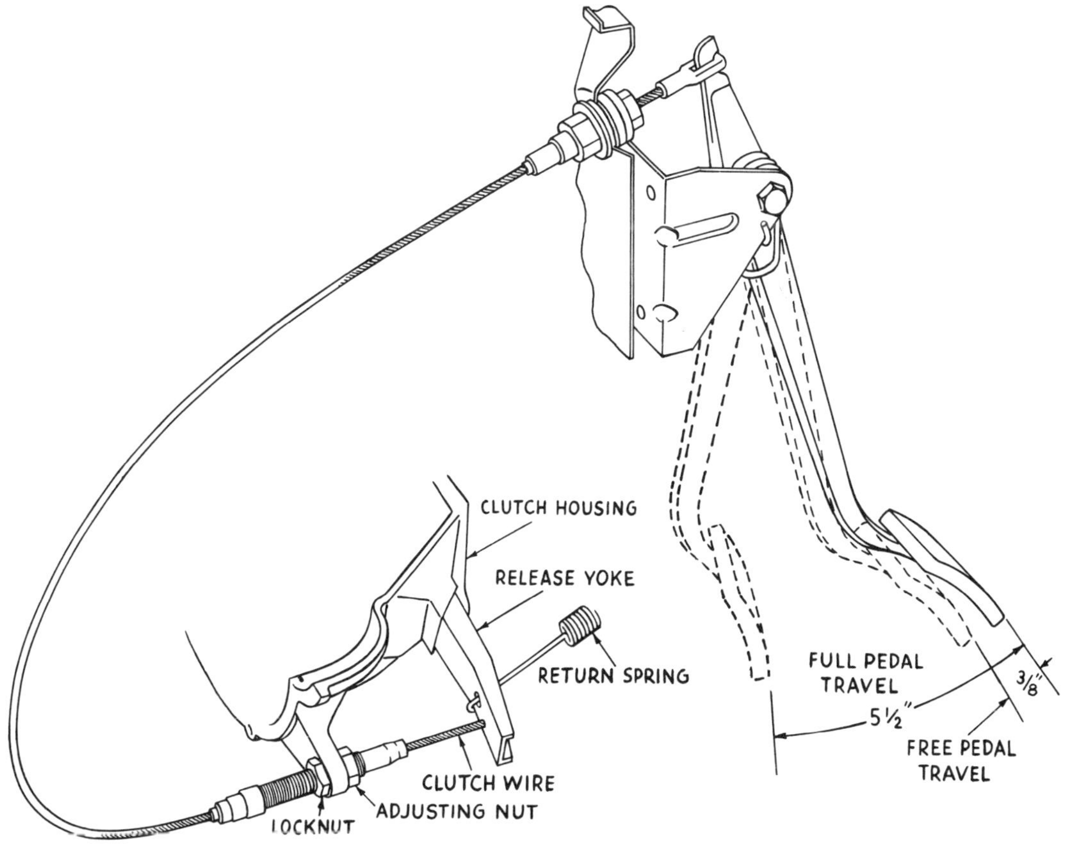

Clutch adjustment, 144.

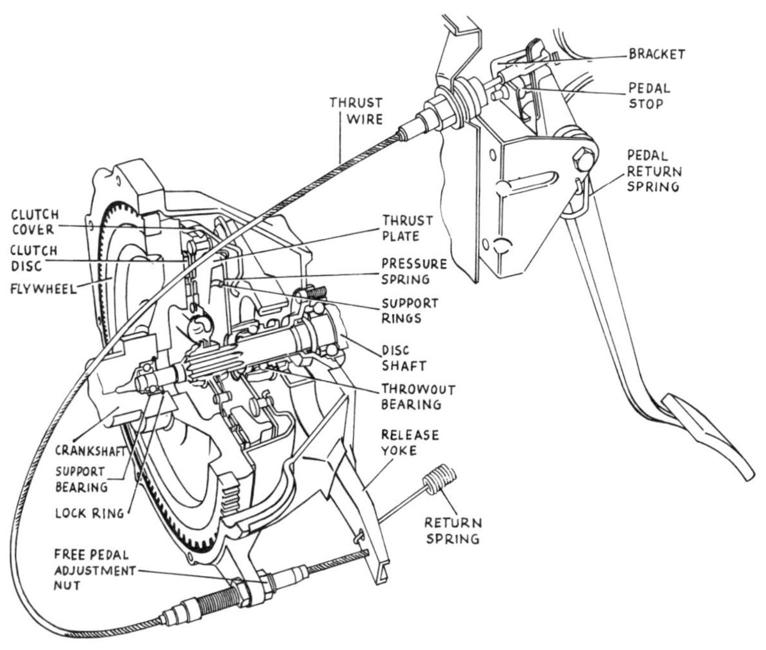

Clutch and clutch controls, 144.

placed. Remove the belt by loosening the generator mount. Tension the new belt by properly positioning the generator. Then tighten the mounting.

Crankcase Ventilation

A positive crankcase ventilation system connects the crankcase with the intake manifold on the engine to return crankcase gases and exhaust blow-by to the combustion chambers for more complete burning. The system consists of an oil trap attached to the valve inspection cover on the right side of the engine (viewed from front) and two rubber hoses between which there is a control valve.

Every 25,000 miles, the hoses, fittings and valve should be cleaned, inspected and replaced if necessary.

Air Cleaner Maintenance

Replace paper filter element on the B18 engine every 12,000 miles under normal driving conditions and more frequently in severe environments. On B20 and B30 engines, replace the insert every 25,000 miles under normal conditions. In dusty or heavily polluted areas replace the insert more often. Do not moisten or oil paper elements. Engines use tons of air even at idle; restriction of air flow inevitably affects engine performance and increases fuel consumption.

Oil-damp type air filters should be washed in solvent, blown dry, and dampened again with oil. Clean every 6,000 miles.

Clutch Pedal Adjustment

All Volvo gear shift models use single dry plate disc type clutches of Borg and Beck manufacture. Clutch control, actuated by the foot pedal, is hydraulic on 122S and 1800S models, mechanical on 164, 144, PV444, 445, 544 and P210 models. The required thrust on the pressure plate is provided by six strong pressure springs on all models except the 164 and 140 which utilize a diaphragm type spring.

Using a short set wrench loosen the locknut, and screw the adjusting nut until free pedal travel is ⅜″ to 19⁄32″ (10-15 mm) and the release yoke has a travel of about ⅛″ to the ball on the clutch wire. Lock the adjusting nut with the locknut after adjustment is reached. Clutch pedal travel should be 5½″ (140 mm).

Brake Check and Adjustment

Check condition of drum brakes by depressing pedal firmly. If pedal travels to within 2 inches of floor mat and has a hard feel, brake shoes require adjustment or relining. Remove wheel, hub and drum assembly to check lining. If worn nearly to rivets, reline brakes. If pedal has a spongy feel, brake system needs bleeding. Check fluid level in master cylinder reservoir and add fluid if necessary. Adjust drum type brakes by jacking up the car so the wheels are free to turn. Release the handbrake. Remove the rubber seal. Turn the wheel in a forward direction of rotation while turning the notched adjuster screw with a screwdriver inserted through the slot in

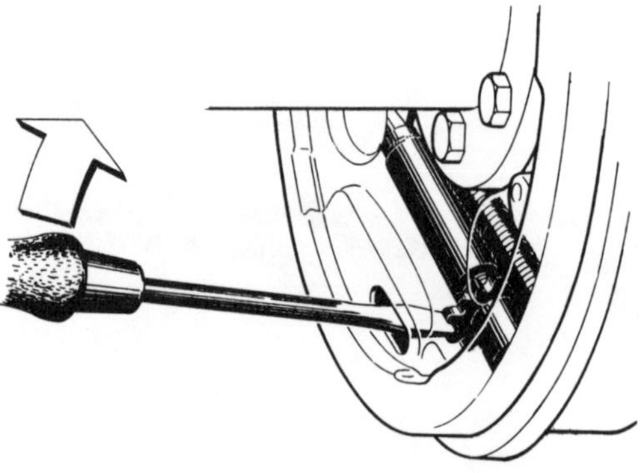

Using screwdriver to adjust brakes.

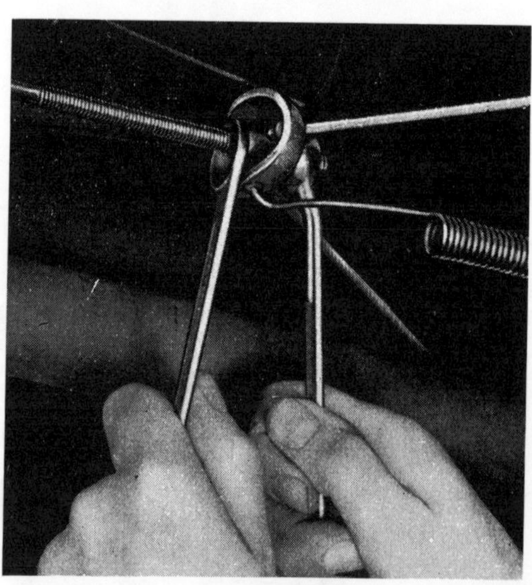

Adjusting handbrake.

the back plate. When the wheel can just be turned using one hand, back off the adjuster screw about 12 notches. Install the rubber seal.

Disc brakes do not require adjustment. However, the friction pads in the calipers must be checked for wear every 6000 miles. Brake pads should be replaced when 1/16″ or less lining remains.

Adjust parking brake when hand lever has a travel greater than ratchet clicks. Fully release hand lever, check cable freedom and loosen equalizer and adjusting nut. Pull lever up three clicks and tighten cable with rear brakes just beginning to bind. Check for equal action at both brakes. Lubricate cable.

Fuses

The fuse block is located either on the left front under the hood or on the heater element below the dash. If an electrical circuit blows a fuse, a new fuse should be installed after the cause of the trouble has been eliminated. A few spare fuses of the correct rating are good protection in emergencies.

Wheel and Tire Care

Wheel and Tire Balance

Wheel and tire balance is more critical with respect to tire wear than casual drivers realize. Unbalance is the principal cause of tramp, car shake, pounding and riding roughness. It often contributes to steering misalignment and damage.

Original balance of the tire and wheel is gradually lost as the tires wear. Severe acceleration, braking, cornering and sideslipping upset wheel balance in even less

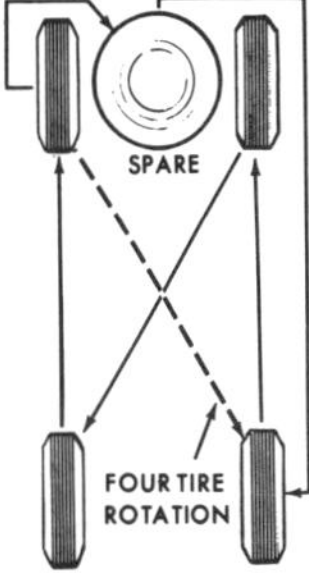

Broken line shows tire rotation pattern when not using spare.

Excessive wear along tire edges was caused by prolonged underinflation.

Excessive wear along center of tire tread was caused by prolonged overinflation.

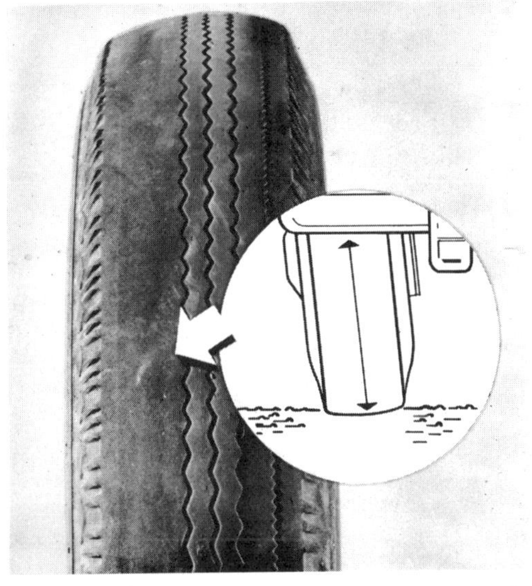

Improper camber caused tire to wear on one side.

Abnormal wear across entire tread surface is a result of front end misalignment. If tread design wears in spots, the wheel is most likely out of balance.

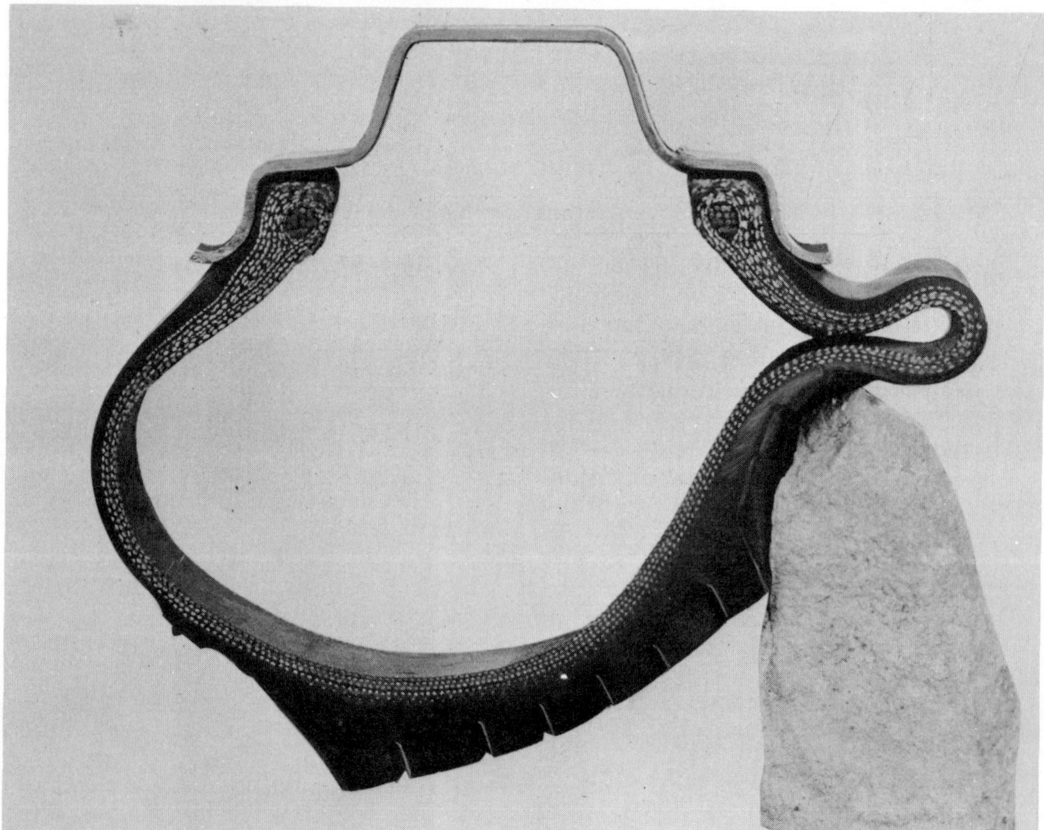

Bruise damage occurs from striking a rock or curb, particularly if the blow is to the sidewall area.

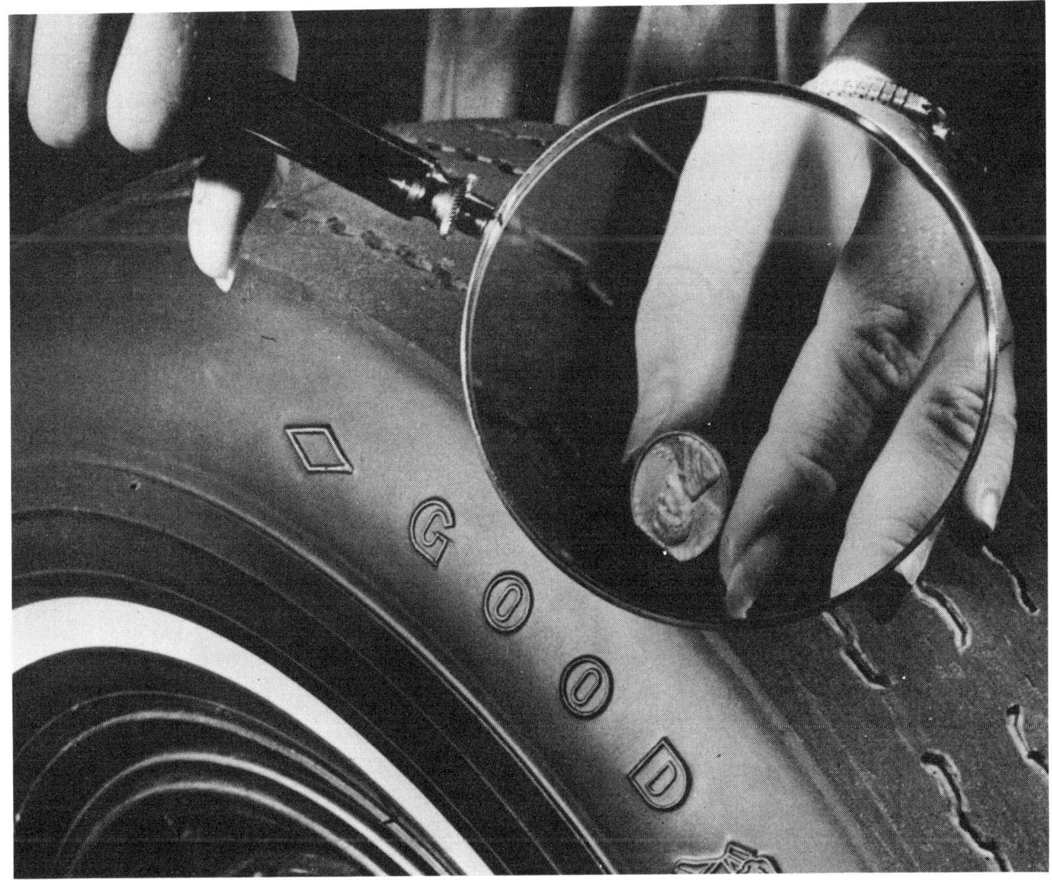

A simple test for tread life. If the head of the figure is partially covered, there is sufficient tread remaining for safety. Tires should be replaced if, as shown, coin can hardly be inserted in groove.

time. Wheels also need balancing after punctures are repaired.

Check wheel balance each time the tires are rotated—every 6000 miles—for maximum tire and front end life.

Tire Wear and Storage Notes

Tread design is one of the more important considerations in tire performance. The design affects acceleration, speed, cornering, braking, heat dissipation, wear, noise and related factors. Necessarily, tread pattern should be checked periodically for premature wear to a dangerous point.

Check tread life by placing a penny in a tread groove. If the top of Lincoln's head is completely exposed, the tire should be replaced or recapped. Ninety percent of tire failure occurs in the last 10% of tread life. A more convenient tread wear indicator is the solid crossbars of rubber that show across the tire when the tread pattern has worn to 1/16″ of an inch. These bars are now required by Federal legislation for all tires.

Storage Tips

To avoid shortening service life, tires must be properly stored while they are not in use. These tips will help keep stored tires in good condition.

1. Check the tires for road damage. Remove stones and other objects that may be trapped in the tread grooves. Have any necessary repairs made.

2. Store the tires in a clean, dry, cool, closed and dark room.

3. Keep the tires away from water, petroleum products such as gasoline and oil, electric motors and heat sources.

4. Place the tires on their sidewalls on a flat surface; permanent flat-spotting can result if the tires are stored standing on their treads.

5. Inflation pressure should be reduced to 12 to 16 pounds if tires are to be stored mounted on wheels.

6. White sidewall tires should be placed whitewall to whitewall, one on top of the other, to protect the white rubber from scuffs and dirt.

Tire Sizes and Pressures

Model	*Inflation Pressure (PSI)*			*Rim Cross-sec. (in.)*	*Tire Size*
	Normal Load		*Heavy Loads*		
	Front	*Rear*	*Rear*		
122, 122S	21	23	28	4	5.90 x 15
PV444	18	21	26		–
PV544	20	23	26	4	6.00 x 15
P1800, 1800S	26	28			6.85 x 15 or 165SR-15
142, 144, 145				4.5	6.00 x 15 or 165-15
164				4.5	6.85 x 15 or 165SR-15

General Dimensions

Model	*Overall Dimensions (in.)*			*Ground Clear-ance*	*Weight (lbs.)*
	Length	*Width*	*Height*		
164	186	68.3	56.7	7.0	2992
145	182.7	68.3	56.7	8.3	2702
144, 142	182.7	68.3	57.0	8.3	2600
1800	173.25	66.9			2460
145S	181	68.3	57.0	8.3	
144, 142	182.7	68.3	56.7	6.3	2640
1800S	173.25	66.9			2460
PV-544C	175	62.5	61.5	7.5	
122S	175	63.5	59.2	7.7	2366
P-1800	173	67	51	5.3	2430
122	175	63.5	59.2	7.7	2366
PV-544	175	62.5	61.5	7.5	

Locating No-Start Problems

When the cause of the engine failure is uncertain, the most efficient way to get the engine running smoothly again is to follow a series of troubleshooting checks that break no-start problems into four areas—engine-cranking, ignition, fuel and compression. Locating the no-start trouble is easily done by following this simple sequence.

1. First try to crank the engine with the starter. Slow engine cranking, or none at all, indicates that the trouble is in the battery, cables, switches or starter. Detailed testing to find the specific defect is provided in the next section of this chapter, *Testing No-Start Components,* ENGINE CRANKING SYSTEM CHECKS.

2. If engine-cranking checked out normal, disconnect a wire from a spark plug, hold it (avoid shock by wearing glove) about ¼ to ½-inch from the plug terminal, and have the engine cranked over with the ignition switched on. Check for strong, evenly timed arcs. The ignition system must supply (often through worn parts) an amount of voltage necessary to form a bright spark at the electrode gap. If there is no spark or if the arc pulse is irregular or weak, the problem is in the ignition system. Special testing to identify ignition malfunctions is described in the next section, under IGNITION.

3. With cranking and ignition successfully checked, remove the air cleaner for access to the carburetor(s). Work the throttle linkage up and down. A stream of fuel should spurt from the accelerator jet(s). If no fuel ejects into the carburetor throat(s) after repeated throttle pumping, there is a defect in the fuel system. A less-common malfunction is continuous flooding of the carburetor(s). If the carb throats are soaked with gasoline and fumes are profuse, have the motor cranked and check for fuel streaming from the main jet(s) into the intake manifold. This check reveals another type of fuel system trouble. Extensive testing procedures are presented in the next section, under FUEL.

4. The last no-start troubleshooting check is for an infrequent, yet sometimes elusive problem—no compression. In most cases, compression failures show up in one

or two cylinders, and are normally not severe enough to prevent starting. However, having no compression in all cylinders will prevent starting. Complete compression failures can be caused by a jumped timing chain, a burnt valve, a broken camshaft, or possibly, the improper mating of timing gears in a newly rebuilt engine. Check for compression by removing a spark plug, sealing the piston chamber with a thumb, cork or other object, and having the engine cranked over. Good compression will gently pop the thumb from the opening. No-compression troubles are analyzed in another section, *Hard Starting, Poor Performance–Tuning.*

Testing No-Start Components

Once the no-start problem has been localized to one of the areas—engine-cranking, ignition, fuel, compression–special testing within that area can directly identify the malfunction while saving expense and valuable time. Each of the units below has a step-by-step troubleshooting test procedure to eliminate suspicion of working parts and to determine the exact trouble.

Engine Cranking System Checks

The engine-cranking network includes the battery, cables, switches and starter. The battery and cables are checked first because they are the storehouse and supply of all electrical power . . . . feeding the starter motor, ignition system, lights, and accessories.

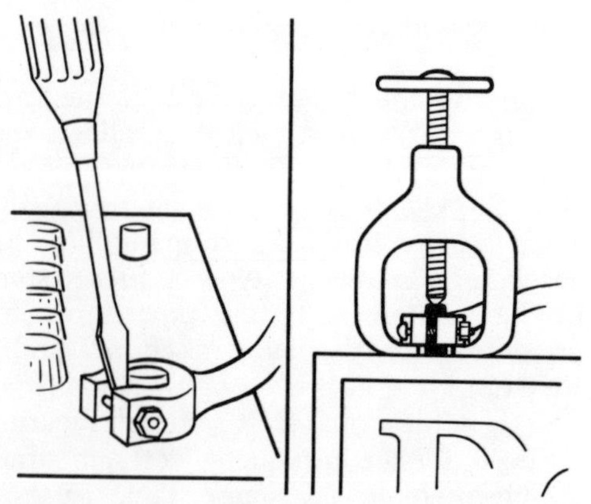

Spreading cable clamp and pulling it from battery terminal.

Turn on the headlights and crank the engine with the starter. If the lights dim out sharply and the cranking slows drastically, either the battery cables are making poor contact or the battery itself is nearly discharged.

If the headlights stay bright but the starter turns slowly or does not turn over, the starter cables or switches may be faulty or the starter defective. Check the difference in voltage readings taken at the battery and at the starter while the starter is cranking the engine to determine the voltage drop through the cables and solenoid.

Checking Cables

Check the connections by carefully working a screwdriver between each cable connector and its terminal post. WARNING: *Hammering, jarring or prying against the terminal may loosen and short-out the battery plates.* If engine cranking improves, the trouble is the connection. Sometimes an imperfect connection can be identified simply by "smoke" or vapor rising from corrosion in that area when the starter switch is actuated.

Cleaning cables and terminals should be done with utmost care to prevent damage to the battery. If a cable cannot be removed by hand easily after the clamp bolt is loosened, a small screw-type puller should be used.

Thorough wire brushing or application of a strong baking soda solution will successfully clean terminals and connectors. CAUTION: *cleaning solution will damage the battery cells if allowed to seep through the vented caps.*

Battery Test

If engine fails to crank after checking out the cable connections, the battery is discharged. A hydrometer reading can quickly tell if any cells are dead. A battery that is normal (though discharged) will have nearly equal specific gravity readings for each cell. (Readings of a fully charged battery range from 1.280 to 1.310, depending on the make.) But if one or two cells have a reading far lower than the others, there is an electrical short circuit within the battery. Tips for charging batteries prop-

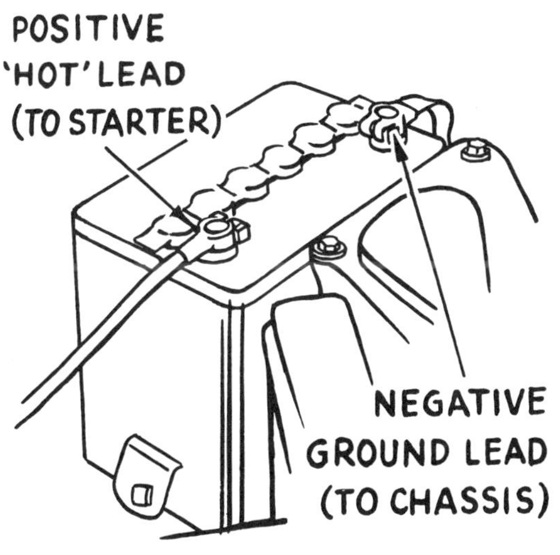

Battery connections.

erly are given in Chapter I under Battery Care.

Once it has been determined that the battery is discharged, the generator and regulator must be checked for the proper charging rate. The electrical system is investigated in Chapter 5.

Testing Generator and Regulator

After checking condition and tension of fan belt, turn off all accessories, set engine speed up to around 2500 rpm, and attach ammeter in series with regulator and battery by disconnecting red lead from "B+" regulator terminal and adding ammeter between terminal and red wire. Output must be 20 amperes minimum on a 12-volt generator and 50 amperes on a 6-volt D.C. unit (at 2000 rpm). A lower

Electrical Specifications

Engine	Battery			Starter					Brush Spring Tension (lbs.)
				Lock Test		No Load Test			
	Capacity (amp. hrs.)	Voltage (volts)	Grounded Terminal	Amps	Volts	Amps	Volts	RPM	
B-14, B-16	85	6	Neg	450-500	3.5	60-80	5.5	4,000-5,000	1.75-2.00
B-18, B-20, B-30	60	12	Neg	300-350	6	40-50	12	6,900-8,100	2.53-2.86

Engine	Generator				Regulator				
						Cut-out Relay			
	Part Number	Brush Spring Pressure (lbs.)	Field Resistance (ohms)	Max. Output (amps)	Part Number	Cuts in at (volts)	Reverse Current at (amps)	Max. Current (amps)	Voltage Regulator Setting (volts)
B-18	Bosch LJ/ GG240/12/ 2400/AR6 or 7	1.0-1.3	4.8±0.5	30	Bosch RS/ VA240/12/ 12	12.4-13.1	2.0-7.5	45 cold 30 warm	14.1-14.8 idling, 13.0-14.0 loaded

Engine	Alternator			Regulator	
	Part Number	Output (amps) at rpm	Minimum Brush Length (in.)	Part Number	Voltage (volts) at alt. rpm, cold
B-20	Bosch K1(R)-14V, 35A20	35 @ 1,200	.32	Bosch AD-14V	14.0-15.0 @ 4,000
B-30	S.E.V. Motorola 14V-26641	30 @ 1,500	.20	S.E.V. Motorola 14V-33525	13.1-14.4 cold, 13.85-14.25 hot

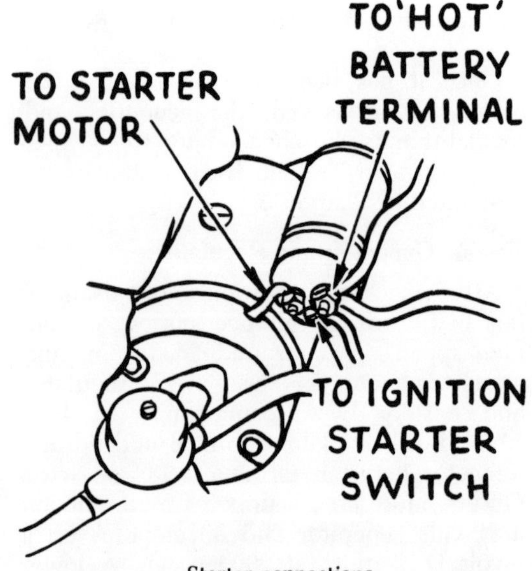

Starter connections.

output indicates malfunction in the generator or regulator. Identify the cause by disconnecting the generator field lead from the regulator and connecting it to the generator armature terminal. If output is still low, generator is faulty. Replace as in Chapter Five. If not, continue tests.

Remove red battery lead from regulator "B+" terminal and connect voltmeter positive lead to this terminal. Run voltmeter negative lead to ground. Increase engine speed until voltage peaks within 13.5–14.5 range. Six-volt regulator limits voltage to 7.0–7.5 volts.

If voltage reading is not in range, remove regulator cover and adjust voltage regulator armature spring tension to obtain a middle reading of 14.0 volts. If reading fluctuates, voltage contacts are dirty.

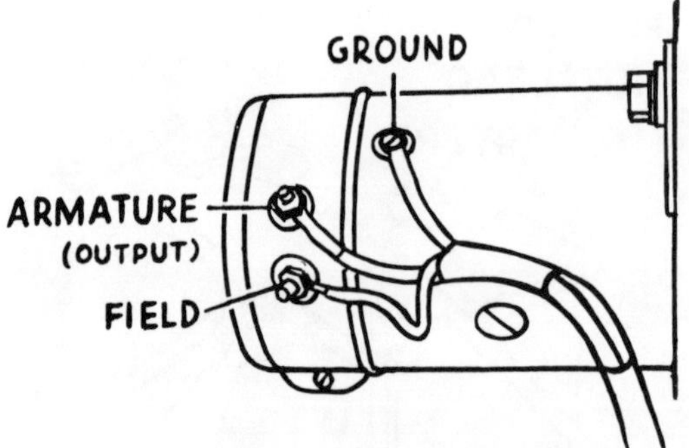

Generator connections.

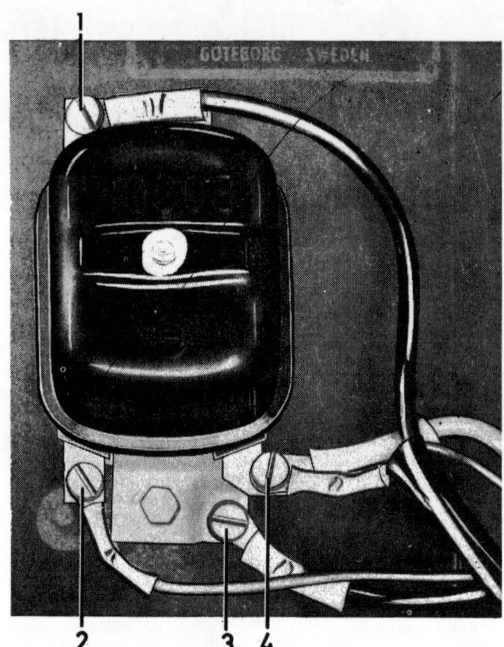

1. B+, to battery "hot" terminal
2. DF, to generator field
3. Ground
4. D+, to generator armature

Regulator connections.

Cutout Relay Closing Voltage—DC Regulator

Connect voltmeter positive lead to regulator "61" (lower rear) terminal. Attach negative lead to ground. Connect ammeter in series with "B+" (upper rear) terminal and disconnect red wire to battery. Increase engine speed and observe voltage increase (until cutout relay points close) and then drop slightly as circuit is completed to battery. The highest voltmeter reading before the drop is the closing voltage. Closing voltage: 12.3–13.2 volts; 5.9 to 6.5 volts. If closing voltage is not within limits, adjust closing voltage by bending cutout relay spring support. Increase spring tension to increase closing voltage—decrease spring tension to decrease closing voltage.

Generator and regulator removal and repair are described in Chapter Five.

Testing the Alternator and Regulator

Bosch—Alternator Test

Connect the alternator as shown in the test diagram and run the engine at 1000

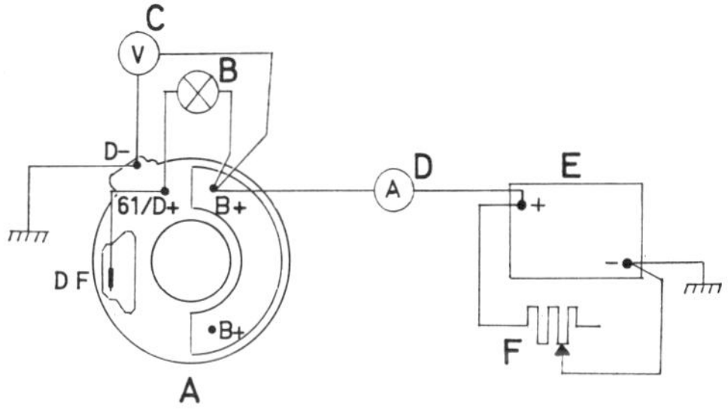

A. Alternator
B. Control lamp, 12 volts, 2 watts
C. Voltmeter, 0–20 volts
D. Ammeter, 0–50 amps
E. Battery
F. Load resistance

Wiring diagram for testing Bosch alternator.

rpm, until the alternator is warm (about 140°F). It should then produce at least 23 amps at 14 volts. Adjust the voltage by means of the load resistance. Increase engine speed to 2000 rpm and check that the test and warning lights do not light. If the alternator does not meet the above specifications, check the brush holder and diodes.

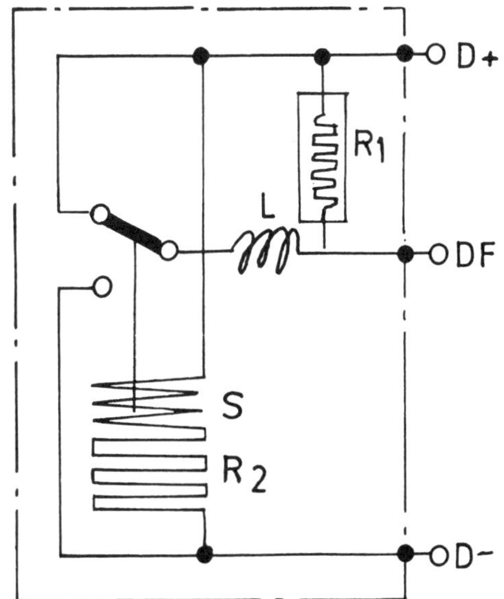

S—Voltage winding, 35 ohms
R_1—Regulator resistance, 2.45 ohms
R_2—Compensation resistance, 50 ohms
L—Contact impedence coil

Inner wiring of Bosch AC voltage regulator.

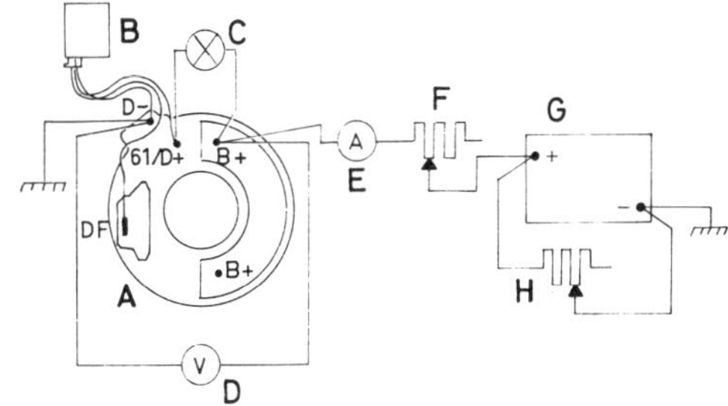

A. Alternator
B. Voltage regulator
C. Control lamp, 12 volts, 2 watts
D. Voltmeter, 0–20 volts
E. Ammeter, 0–50 amps
F. Control resistance
G. Battery
H. Load resistance

Wiring diagram for testing Bosch AC voltage regulator.

Bosch—Voltage Regulator Test

Connect the voltage regulator as shown in the test diagram and run the engine at 2000 rpm. Load the alternator with 28 to 30 amps. Lower the engine speed to idle, raise it again to 2000 rpm and adjust the load to 28 to 30 amps. The voltage should now be 14 to 15 volts. Adjustments should be made on the left (lower) contact.

Reduce the load to 3 to 8 amps. The voltage should now be between minus 0.9 and plus 0.2 volts of the first reading.

Lower range adjustments are made by bending the stop clamp. Bending up raises the voltage and bending down lowers the voltage.

Motorola—Voltage Drop Test

With a 10 amp load (headlights, for instance) the voltage drop between the B+ pole of the alternator and the positive pole of the battery should be less than 0.3 volts, and between the D— pole of the alternator and the negative pole of the battery should be less than 0.2 volts. If there is a greater drop, check the wiring and the ground connection.

Alternator Test

Connect the alternator as shown in the test diagram. Check that the current through the field is 2 to 2.5 amps. With the engine running at 1400 rpm, the alternator should deliver at least 30 amps at about 13 volts. Compare the voltage at the B+ pole

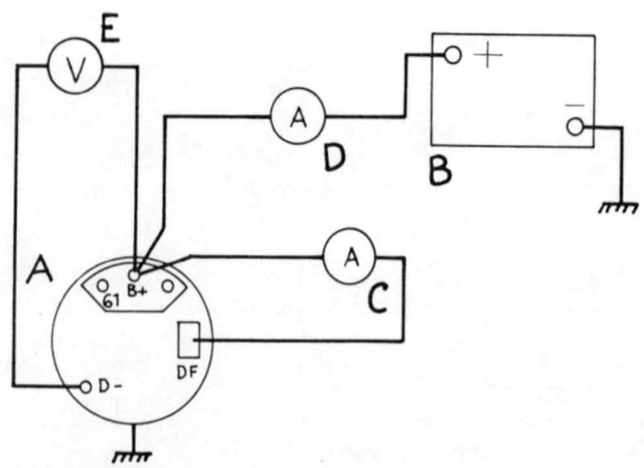

A. Alternator
B. Battery
C. Ammeter, 0–10 amps
D. Ammeter, 0–50 amps
E. Voltmeter, 0–20 volts

Wiring diagram for testing Motorola alternator.

and terminal 61. Voltage should be 0.8 to 0.9 volts higher at terminal 61, otherwise the isolation diode is faulty.

Voltage Regulator Test

Connect the voltage regulator as shown in test diagram. Run the engine at 2300 rpm for 15 seconds. The voltage at the voltmeter should be 13.1 to 14.4 volts with the alternator at 75°F (25°C).

Switch on the headlights (to give a load of about 10 to 15 amps). The voltage should be between 13.1 and 14.4 volts at about 75°F (25°C). If the voltage exceeds the tolerances, the voltage regulator should be replaced.

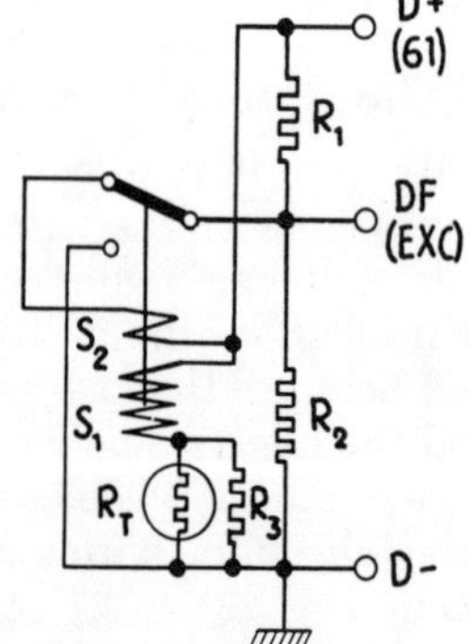

S_1 Voltage winding
S_2 Accelerator winding
R_1 Regulator resistance, 10 ohms ± 10%
R_2 Damper resistance, 30 ohms ± 10%
R_3 Compensation resistance (adapted to RT during manufacture)
RT Compensation thermistor, approximately 4 ohms at 75° F. (25° C.)

Motorola AC voltage regulator inner circuit.

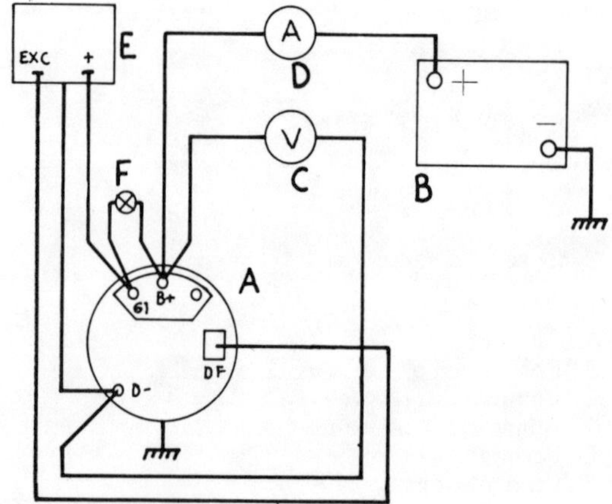

A. Alternator
B. Battery
C. Voltmeter, 0–20 volts
D. Ammeter, 0–50 amps
E. Voltage regulator
F. Test light, 12 volts, 2 watts

Wiring diagram for testing Motorola AC voltage regulator.

Checking Switches

After the battery and cables have been checked, the starting system switches should be tested.

(Test 1) First, bypass the starter switch by running a jump cable or other heavy-gauge lead directly from the positive terminal of the fully charged battery to the input terminal of the solenoid. (DANGER: Rings, watches and other metal in contact with the hand can cause severe burns with accidental battery-voltage contact. A heavy-cloth glove offers good protection against burns caused by sudden overheating of the jump cable.) If the starter motor comes to life when the electrical contact is made, the malfunction is in the starter switch or its wiring. If there is no starter response or just a click in the solenoid, make a second test.

(Test 2) Cautiously touch the hot cable directly to the starting motor input lead. This bypasses the solenoid. In a clutch-type starter assembly, the starter should spin but will not engage the flywheel when the solenoid is omitted from the circuit. If the starter spins, the trouble is in the solenoid unless the solenoid had clicked in the previous test. The solenoid serves two simultaneous functions—switching power into the starting motor and engaging the starter-clutch assembly. If the

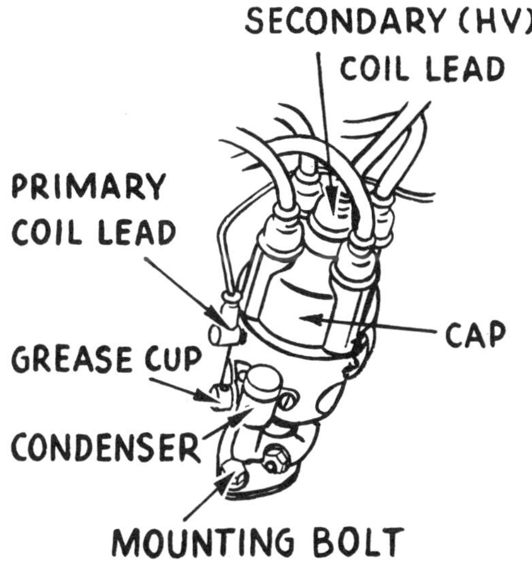

Distributor components.

solenoid clicked in the first test and the starting motor spun free in the second test, the solenoid is good and the trouble is a locked or frozen engine. (If starter gear is jammed against flywheel, place transmission in high gear and gently rock car back and forth.) Getting no response with the hot lead on the starter terminal indicates that the problem is in the starting motor itself.

Starter Check

The intensity of the spark at the contact of the hot cable with the starter input may help determine the fault in the motor. A bright, nearly-welding flash indicates that there is a shorted circuit within the starting motor. A weak spark or none at all points to a poor connection of the motor brushes with the commutator. The brushes could be completely worn. The brush springs could be broken. The commutator could have burnt spots or be dirty or oily.

Chapter 5 provides detailed overhaul procedures for electrical equipment as well as procedures for testing assemblies with a voltmeter.

Ignition

Troubleshooting the ignition system for a no-start problem involves checking through the primary and secondary ignition circuits from the battery to the spark plugs. Locating the shorted circuit can be done quickly by following the easy tests below.

The initial test for troubleshooting the ignition system was to check for the strength and pulse of the arc between a disconnected spark plug wire to its terminal ¼ to ½-inch away. A poor spark indicated ignition system trouble. (Locating No-Start Problems)

Testing Ignition Switch

Ignition switch failures are the most frequent so are wisely checked first. Find the wire from the ignition switch that leads to the ignition coil, disconnect it at the coil and turn on the ignition. Touch the detached wire momentarily to a ground. Watch for a faint spark. No spark indicates a failure in the switch or in wiring or connections between the battery and the coil. If the wire did spark when touched to a ground, reconnect it to the coil before proceeding.

Checking Coil Circuit

Though the coil supplies electrical power to the distributor cap and from there to the spark plugs, it is energized and timed by the contact points inside the distributor. Therefore, checking the coil also requires testing the points.

First remove the distributor cap. Check it and the distributor rotor (on the shaft below the cap) for fractures and worn metal parts. Check the center carbon contact (button) in the distributor cap. The button should extend from the cap, be clean and have no cracks.

Turn the engine by hand slowly (grasping the fan belt and pulley) until the contact points are fully apart. After removing the high-tension coil lead from the distributor cap (center wire), turn on the ignition switch. With a small screwdriver, firmly short-circuit the movable contact point to the fixed contact point while holding the disconnected high-tension wire approximately ¼ inch from a ground. Repeated contact and breaking of the circuit with the screwdriver should give an intermittent spark from the high-tension wire to ground. A weak spark, or none at all, means there is a bad ignition coil or faulty wiring between the distributor points and the coil.

Inspection of Contact Points

While the contact points are still positioned fully apart, make checks to determine if they should be cleaned or replaced or if the condenser is bad.

First, inspect the points for pits and discoloration. Second, with the ignition switched on, firmly slide a screwdriver slowly down the side of the movable contact almost to the base of the distributor. As the screwdriver gets closer, electricity should arc to the base. If there is no spark or the spark is not strong and distinct, the problem is in the condenser or in the distributor wiring.

Next, have the engine cranked by the starter while closely observing the opening and closing of the contact points. An arc should occur between the points just as they begin to break contact. Again the spark must be strong and distinct. Poor arcing shows that the points should be cleaned or replaced. No arcing indicates that the wiring within the distributor is faulty or the condenser is bad.

If these two tests showed no sparking across the contact points, inspect the primary and ground wiring in the distributor and then test the condenser.

Primary Circuit Wiring Check

The coil primary wire that attaches (within the condenser) to the contact-point assembly terminal sometimes becomes twisted, frayed, or shorted (often intermittently) to the housing. Another problem could be a broken ground (pigtail) wire between the contact-point assembly plate and the distributor housing. Closely inspect the wiring for faults.

Condenser Check

Detach and isolate the condenser housing from the distributor while leaving the condenser lead on its terminal. Hand-turn the engine to open the points fully and then short-out the movable contact point by slowly sliding the screwdriver (against the contact) down toward the distributor base. If the spark occurs across the gap between the screwdriver and ground, the condenser has a short-circuit and must be replaced. To test out a condenser positively is difficult to do and perhaps not worth the time. It is best to replace a suspected condenser.

Fuel System Checks

Troubleshooting the fuel system for starting problems normally requires a check of the carburetors, fuel pump, tank and fuel lines for fuel restriction. A less common no-start problem is chronic carburetor flooding.

Checking Carburetors

In the previous section *(Locating No-Start Problems)*, the throttle linkage was worked up and own by hand to check fuel ejection into the carb throats by the accelerator jets. No-start fuel problems most often involve the situation in which no gasoline reaches the carburetors.

In rare instances, *stale* gasoline will prevent starting. To test for stale fuel, prime the engine by squirting fresh gas into the carb throats. If the engine kicks over—analyze the gas in the tank by removing a small sample to a distant, safe area and cautiously attempt to ignite it.

If there is no fuel at the carburetors, check the tank, lines and fuel pump. First, look for an improperly vented cap. Remove gas cap and attempt to start engine. If it starts, cap is improperly vented. Just in case the gauge has failed, next check for gasoline in the tank, by shaking car and listening for sloshing sound.

Fuel Pump Test

If lacking gas at the carburetor, disconnect the fuel pump outlet line. WARNING: *to safeguard against dangerous sparks, first remove the high tension coil-distributor wire.* Cranking the engine should force fuel out of the line in steady spurts. A further test is to disconnect the input line of the fuel pump, hold a thumb on the input fitting while cranking the engine, and test for suction from the pump. No suction indicates that the fuel-pump diaphragm is leaking—maybe perforated—or that the diaphragm linkage is worn. Check the crankcase for gasoline. Often a ruptured diaphragm will leak fuel into the engine. A broken or worn cam shaft or cam lobe could also be the defect.

Checking Tank and Lines

Good suction at the pump input indicates a restricted fuel line to the tank or a clogged tank filter. Drain tank, blow compressed air through the line from the fuel pump, and then flush tank.

Test for Vapor Lock

Fuel lines in areas exposed to excessive heat should be insulated because gasoline vaporizes when heated. The vapor bubbles prevent fuel flow to the carburetors and thus starve the engine for gas. If vapor forms and stalls the engine, let it cool if possible before trying to restart it.

Hard Starting, Poor Performance—Tuning

Many who have the "If it works, don't fool with it" attitude find that when they have car trouble, it is a major and expensive problem. A smarter approach that assures maximum car enjoyment is to keep an alert eye and ear on the car's daily performance. In addition, a semi-annual tune-up (Spring, Autumn) most economically maintains good performance.

A thorough tune-up should include a close inspection of the major mechanical parts and lubricating system of the engine as well as the normal electrical and fuel system overhaul. Ideal instruments for quickly checking mechanical engine parts are compression and vacuum gauges and a short piece of hose (a makeshift stethoscope).

These devices and other simple tools are used in the following step-by-step troubleshooting and tune-up procedures.

Spark Plugs and Wiring Check

After removing the spark plugs, carefully inspect them for cracked or broken porcelain and loose electrodes. Compare the condition of the spark plugs to that of the plugs illustrated to identify the cause of poor performance. In general, the symptoms are indicated by the color of the plugs: tan or medium gray—proper carburetion, plug in good working order; black—fuel mixture too rich, gap too wide, plug too cold; light gray—fuel mixture too lean, plug loose or leaking, valves not closing fully, plug too hot. Oily plugs might indicate that oil has been sucked into combustion chamber due to worn cylinders or piston rings or improper crankcase venting. Also possible, if only one or two plugs are affected, is plug misfiring from poor or broken electrical circuit.

Spark plugs with minor carbon and oxide deposits can be cleaned, adjusted and reinstalled. Clean the plugs in a sandblasting machine or carefully by hand with a fine wire brush taking care not to scratch the porcelain. Dry carbon dust is best blown off with compressed air; oily plugs can be washed with a solvent.

Set the electrode gap by bending the outside electrode to the proper clearance. Never bend the center electrode. See specifications for spark plug types and recommended gaps.

Spark plugs should not be reset more than once because the point-of-heat changes as the center electrode wears back toward the insulator. Place a new compression gasket on each plug and tighten with only enough force to crush the gasket (normally ½ turn after seated by hand).

Wiring

Spark plug wiring should be removed, cleaned with a kerosene-moistened cloth, wiped dry and then carefully inspected for brittle, cracked, gummy or otherwise deteriorated insulation. Aged wiring permits electrical spark leakage . . . the cause of engine misses and crossfiring. Defective wiring should be replaced. Inspect and clean the wire terminals, spark plug terminals, and the distributor cap sockets to assure perfect electrical contact.

Distributor

After removing the distributor cap, inspect it for carbon paths which accumulate in areas of high voltage leakage. Discard the cap if any are present. Otherwise, clean the inside of the cap and check for cracks. Remove corrosion from the copper contacts and inspect the condition of the center (carbon) button. The button should extend from the cap, be clean and without cracks. If any contacts are deeply scored, replace the cap.

Inspect the distributor rotor for burns and, if necessary, replace it. With the rotor arm off, lubricate the distributor cam with non-corrosive high temperature grease. (NOTE: do not allow grease or dirt to contaminate breaker points.) De-

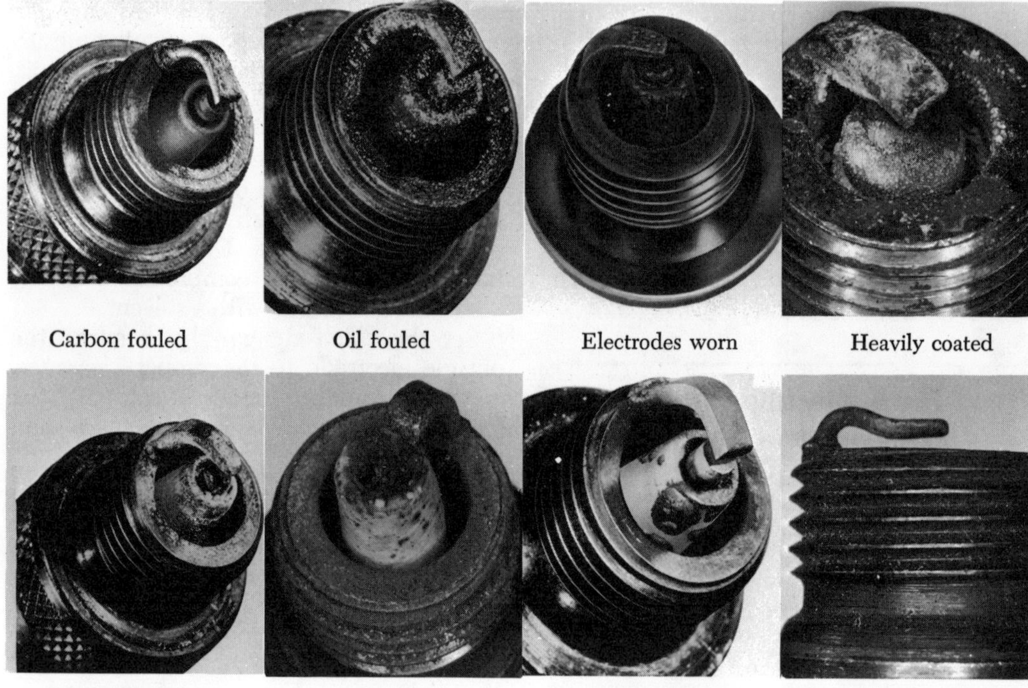

Carbon fouled | Oil fouled | Electrodes worn | Heavily coated

Overheated | Melted | Splash fouled | Bent electrode

Carbon Fouled Plugs
If only one plug is carbon fouled and others are normal, check ignition wiring for a break or loose connections. A compression check might indicate mechanical trouble in that cylinder.
If all plugs are sooted, fuel mixture might be too rich, spark gap could be too large, or the plug heat value is too high.

Oil Fouled Plugs
Plugs may have been "drowned" with fuel during cranking. If choke operates properly, fouling could be caused by poor oil control. A hotter plug is needed.

Excessive Electrode Gap
If all plugs have brown-gray deposits and electrode wear from .008″ to .010″ greater than original gap, they are completely worn. Replace entire set.

Heavily Coated Plugs
Heavy deposits, if easily flaked off, result from scavenger additives used in some brands of fuel. Though this accumulation creates heat buildup, its chemical nature causes only minimum electrical shorting. Replacement plugs should have same heat range.

Chipped Insulator
If one or two plugs in a set have chipped insulator tips, severe detonation was the likely cause. Bending the center electrode during gapping can also crack the insulator. Replace with new plugs of the correct gap and heat range. Check for over-advanced timing.

Normal, Usable Plugs
Plugs with evenly-colored light tan or gray deposits and moderate electrode wear (.005 gap growth) can be cleaned, regapped, and reinstalled.

All Plugs Overheated
If set has dead white insulators and badly eroded electrodes (.001″ erosion per 1,000 miles), check ignition timing for over-advance. Install next colder heat range.

One Plug Badly Burned
If one plug in a set has melted electrodes, preignition was likely encountered in that cylinder; check for intake manifold air leaks and possible cross fire. Be sure the one plug is not the wrong heat range.

Mechanical Damage
A broken insulator and bent electrodes result from some foreign object falling into the combustion chamber. If valves overlap, objects can travel from one cylinder to another. Always clean out cylinders to prevent recurrence.

One or Two Plugs "Splashed" Fouled
Some plugs in a relatively new set may have splashed deposits. This may occur after a long-delayed tune-up when accumulated cylinder deposits are thrown against the plugs at high engine rpm. Clean and reinstall these plugs.

Bent Side Electrodes
Improperly gapping plugs will weaken side electrode and alter electrical performance of spark plug.

Tune-Up Specifications

Engine Model	*Spark Plugs* Make, Type	Gap (in.)	*Distributor* Point Dwell (deg.)	Point Gap (in.)	Basic Igni-* tion Timing (deg.) @ r.p.m.	Cranking Compress. Press. (p.s.i.)	*Valves* Intake① Clear. (in.)	Exhaust① Clear. (in.)	Intake④ Opens (deg.)	Idle Speed
B-14	Champion Y4A/J6	.028-.032	47	.018-.022	20 BTDC @ 1,500		.020	.020	0 @ TDC	
B-16A	Bosch W175T3	.028-.032	47-53	.016-.020	19-21 BTDC @ 1,500	135-150	.016	.018	10 BTDC	
B-16B	Bosch W225T3	.028-.032	47-53	.016-.020	21-23 BTDC @ 1,500	142-156	.020	.020	0 @ TDC	
B-18A	Bosch W175T1	.028-.032	59-65	.016-.020	21-23 BTDC @ 1,500	156-185	.016-.018	.016-.018	10 ATDC	500-700
B-18B	Bosch W225T1	.028-.032	59-65	.016-.020	17-19 BTDC @ 1,500 ③	170-200	.020-.022	.020-.022	0 @ TDC	600-800
B-18D	Bosch W175T1	.028-.032	59-65	.016-.020	22-24 BTDC @ 1,500 ②	156-185	.016-.018	.016-.018	10 ATDC	
B-20A	Bosch W175T35	.028-.032	59-65	.016-.020	21-23 BTDC @ 1,500	156-185	.016-.018	.016-.018	10 ATDC	700
B-20B	Bosch W200T35	.028-.032	59-65	.016-.020	10 BTDC @ 600-800	156-185	.020-.022	.020-.022	0 @ TDC	700
B-30A	Bosch W175T35	.028-.032	37-43	.010	10 BTDC @ 600-800	156-185	.020-.022	.020 .022	0 @ TDC	750

NOTE: Emission control requires a precise approach to tune-up. Timing and idle speed are peculiar to the engine and its application, rather than to the engine alone. Data for the particular application will be found on a sticker in the engine compartment.

*With vacuum line disconnected.

① Either hot or cold.

② Some models with B-18D engines are set at 17-19° BTDC @ 1,500 rpm. Check the owner's manual and engine compartment sticker.

③ B-18B with emission controls – 5° BTDC @ 800 rpm.

④ When checking camshaft setting, adjust valves on cold engine to:

.045	B-16B
.043	B-16A, B-18A, B-18D, B-20A
.057	B-20B, B-30A.

tailed instructions for overhauling the distributor to specifications are given in Chapter 5.

Checking Points, Condenser, Connections

Carefully examine the contact (often called breaker) assemblies in the distributor for the following poor-performance conditions:

1. Points are blackened, pitted, or worn excessively. (Points in extended service normally become dull gray without losing efficiency).
2. Movable contact-point arm has lost spring action.
3. Fiber rubbing block on breaker is badly worn or loose.
4. Coil primary wire (attached to the breaker assembly with the condenser) is twisted, frayed or shorted on the distributor plate.
5. Condenser lead connection is loose or damaged.
6. Ground wire (pigtail) between the breaker assembly plate and the distributor housing is frayed or loose.

If any of the distributor components is faulty, replace it and then identify and repair the fault so that the new part can

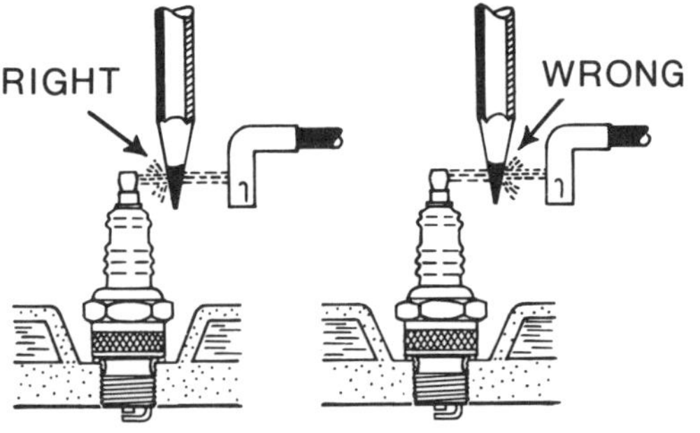

Coil polarity check.

give satisfactory service. Contact points that are slightly burned can be cleaned with a thin cut-stone or point file.

Adjusting Point Gap

The breaker points must be correctly set before adjusting ignition timing. Turn the crankshaft until cam lobe on the distributor shaft has fully raised the breaker arm. Loosen the breaker plate hold-down screw and, using a feeler gauge, adjust the breaker gap to the correct setting by canting a screwdriver in the oval cutout. Then tighten the hold-down screw. Steps for adjusting distributor dwell angle with a dwell meter are listed in Chapter 5.

Coil and Polarity

An ignition coil having reversed polarity could reduce spark plug efficiency as much as 20%. The result would be a drastic loss of power.

Briefly inspect the coil housing for weak spots and cracks (especially around the tower) caused by high-voltage leaks or deterioration.

A check to determine if the ignition polarity matches the negative-to-ground (or positive-to-ground) circuitry of the battery can easily be made in any of three ways.

A. For negative-to-ground systems, firmly attach a "high-reading" voltmeter positive lead to engine ground (connect negative lead to ground for positive-to-ground system). Then, momentarily touch the other lead of the voltmeter to the secondary-circuit coil wire that leads to the distributor cap. A positive (up-scale) voltage reading indicates correct polarity. A negative (down-scale) reading shows a reversed polarity that will cause hard starting and premature wear of ignition components.

B. An optional test is to hold a soft-lead wood pencil in the gap between a disconnected spark plug cable and plug (or ground). With the engine cranking, observe the direction of spark jump between the wire and plug. "Flaring" of spark on the plug side of the pencil means that polarity is correct.

C. "Dishing" on the electrode side indicates wrong polarity. If polarity is wrong, reverse the two primary leads at the ignition coil.

Setting Ignition Timing

If you have not set the breaker point gap, do so before proceeding. See paragraph, *Adjusting Point Gap*.

Next, turn the crankshaft until the Top Dead Center mark on the crankshaft pulley is in line with a raised spot on the timing gear cover. (The B14 and B16 engines have timing marks on the flywheel.) The No. 1 cylinder is in firing position and the distributor rotor should directly face the No. 1 cylinder spark-plug-wire contact in the distributor cap. (A notch in the housing of the distributor indicates that position.)

With TDC marks aligned, follow these steps:

1. Remove the rotor arm.
2. Loosen clamp screw at base of distributor body.
3. Connect a 12-volt test lamp in series between the distributor primary post and a ground.
4. Turn on the ignition.
5. Turn distributor body clockwise until the light goes out (contacts closed), then turn slowly counterclockwise until the exact moment the points open and the light goes on again.
6. Tighten distributor clamp screw.
7. Reinstall rotor arm and distributor cap.
8. Check ignition timing with a strobe light (if available) while engine is idling at 500 rpm and all vacuum hoses are disconnected from the distributor and plugged. Chapter 5 provides detailed steps for setting dwell angle and ignition timing.

Checking Vacuum

The vacuum gauge shows the difference in pressure between the inside and outside of the intake manifold. Since atmospheric pressure varies with altitude and changes daily with the weather, the action of the vacuum gauge needle is more indicative than any specific pressure valve. In general, the vacuum reading is less for higher elevation and also shows a drop from an extreme high-pressure weather system to a stormy, low pressure system. Pressure measurement is in inches. A well-tuned engine will give vacuum readings of between 18 and 20 inches at sea level.

Reading a Vacuum

Attach the gauge to the intake manifold or on the engine side of the carburetor throttle butterfly. Warm the engine, set the idle speed between 800 and 1000 rpms, remove the air filter (in case it is partially clogged) and check to see that the carburetor chokes are open.

Make the first reading with the engine idling around 900 rpm. The needle should be steady and in the 18–20-inch range. If the pointer remains steady but at a substantially lower pressure, the poor performance problem affects power in all of the cylinders. It could be improper ignition or valve timing or an intake manifold leak. Improper valve timing normally gives the indicator a lower reading (7″-drop) than poor ignition timing (4″-drop). The size of a manifold leak determines where the indicator will stabilize. A severe warp or crack may reduce vacuum as much as 15 inches.

If the vacuum indicator wavers or fluctuates at idle rpm, the poor-performance problem normally affects only one or may-

	Vacuum Reading	*Possible Reasons*	*Next Test*
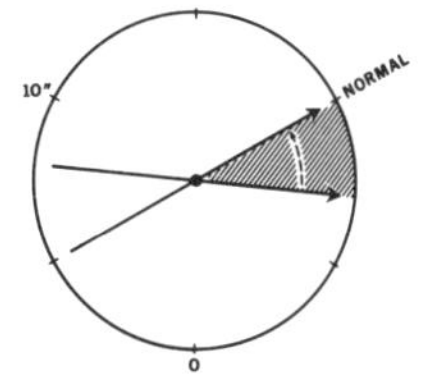 10″ NORMAL 0	Steady gauge reading 18–20″ at all speeds. Throttle is released and engine speed quickly cuts from over 2000 rpm to idle. Needle jumps 2–5″ above normal and then quickly drops to normal without pause or hesitation.	Normal engine performance.	Vacuum okay. Go to compression tests.
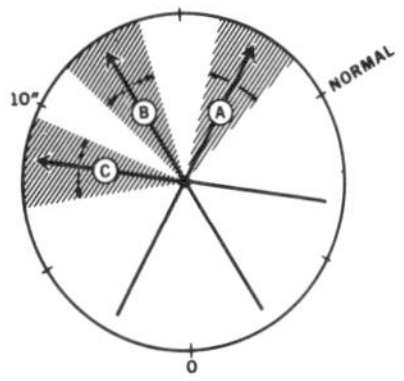 10″ NORMAL A B C 0	Steady low reading. Figure A. (less than 2″ drop)	Retarded ignition timing.	Loosen clamp, rotate distributor to reset timing. Check gauge improvement.
	Steady, very low reading. Figure B.	Late valve timing.	Check valve timing. Make compression tests.
	Steady, extremely low reading. (up to 15″ drop) Figure C.	Severely warped or cracked intake manifold. Bad carburetor-to-manifold gasket.	Inspect manifold. Squirt oil around seal to detect leak.
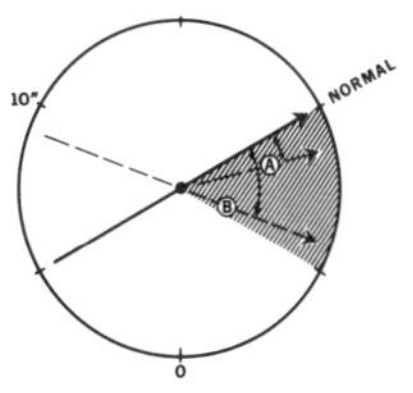 10″ NORMAL A B 0	Pointer does not jump much above normal when throttle is quickly closed and engine speed is cut from above 2000 rpm to idle. Figure A.	Piston rings may be worn or defective and are blowing into crankcase.	Take compression test of cylinders to pinpoint trouble.
	Pointer jumps 2–5″ above normal upon quick deceleration but hesitates at higher pressure before returning to normal. Figure B.	Restricted exhaust system is causing back-pressure on engine.	Check exhaust for dents, restrictions, clogged muffler.

Vacuum Reading	*Possible Reasons*	*Next Test*
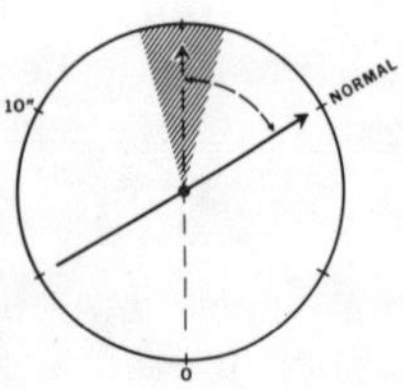 Pointer (rhythmically drops 1–7″ below normal vacuum at regular intervals.	Leaking combustion chamber or valve; (ignition or plug failure involving one cylinder).	Make compression tests; (make ignition check).
Pointer drops rapidly but intermittently (not every time) and then recovers.	Valve sticking at times won't close tight.	Note which valve sticks. Apply penetrating oil to one valve guide at a time. Problem will correct itself temporarily.
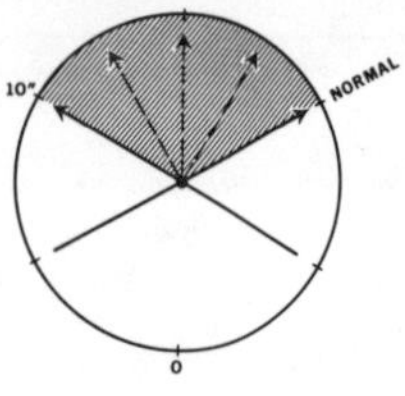 Pointer wavers rapidly between 10–20″ at idle becoming worse with higher rpm.	Weak or broken spring causing valve to close slowly.	Remove valve covers; check condition of springs.
Wavers irregularly at idle; fluctuates rapidly in smaller range at higher rpm.	Manifold leak at intake port—upsets and reduces cylinder draft.	Squirt oil around manifold; check vacuum increase when oil fills leak. Replace faulty gasket.
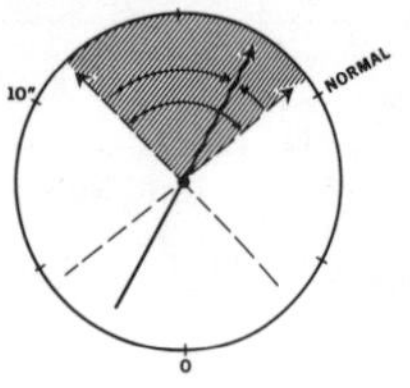 Drifts at idle; stabilizes at higher engine rpm.	Burnt valve; combustion chamber leak.	Make compression tests.
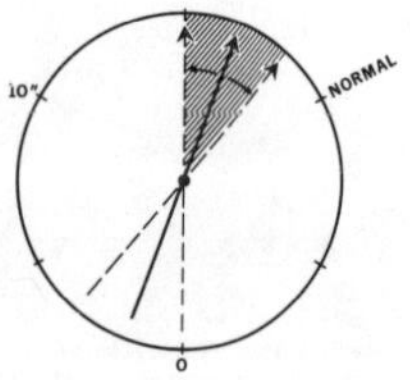 Wavers irregularly in one range despite engine speed.	Unbalanced carburetion; improper spark plug gap, ignition timing; poor valve seating.	Adjust carburetors; check plug gap; check distributor and advance spark; make compression tests.
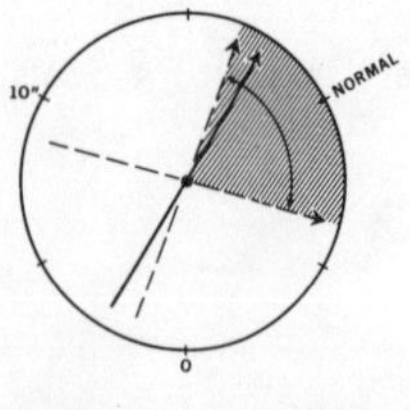 Vacuum averages lower than normal at idle, needle fluctuates almost 3″ on both sides of normal.	Worn valve guides admitting air—upsetting carburetion.	Squirt oil on guide seals. Check vacuum improvement.

be a few cylinders. Use the illustrated guide to interpret vacuum gauge readings.

Checking Compression

A second important instrument is the compression gauge used to measure pressure differences among cylinders. Pressure variations cause loss of power and poor idling.

Warm the engine to hot operating temperature, remove all spark plugs, prop open the throttle linkage so air is not restricted and affix the compression gauge to the spark plug opening.

Crank engine with throttle open and note gauge pointer reading after fifth revolution. Repeat procedure on each cylinder. All cylinders should be within ten pounds of each other and maintain an average pressure of around 150 psi. (See "Tune-up Specifications")

One or two low readings in the cylinders indicate trouble with valves, rings, pistons, or combustion-chamber leaks. Low compression readings in all cylinders indicate incorrect valve timing.

To determine the fault, squirt an ounce (approx.) of light oil into the low-compression cylinder, replace the compression gauge, and crank the engine another five revolutions for the second reading. If compression increases substantially, the rings are worn or stuck and need replacing.

No increase in compression after adding oil to the cylinder narrows the trouble to improper valve seating, a cracked or broken piston, or a combustion-chamber leak between the head and the cylinder.

First, check out the possibility of a combustion-chamber leak. Turn the engine while checking for hissing noises and perhaps a discharge of oil from the flange between the cylinder and the head. This indicates a poor seal between the cylinder head and the cylinder. A leaky head gasket can often be detected by loss of compression in two adjacent cylinders.

Detecting piston damage involves replacing all the spark plugs, starting the engine, and listening for a distinctive clicking noise at idle and upon acceleration. Combustion gasses (blow-by) will also escape into the crankcase through the piston crack. See TROUBLESHOOTING ENGINE NOISES, in this chapter.

Abnormal Oil Consumption

Another way to identify poor-performance troubles is a check of oil consumption. Continual addition of oil, fouled spark plugs and blue-gray exhaust smoke are obvious signs.

Worn or broken piston rings permit oil to enter the combustion-chamber and reduce burning efficiency. In addition, poor rings permit combustion gases to enter the crankcase. This hot "blow-by" changes the crankcase oil into vapor that escapes through the ventilating system. Blow-by also pressurizes the crankcase, forcing oil leakage through the weak pan seals.

Worn valve guides fail to keep oil out of the combustion-chamber, resulting in poor performance and excessive oil consumption. Piston ring and valve guide replacement steps are detailed in Chapter 3.

Before assuming that engine wear is the cause of excessive oil usage, make a thorough inspection for external leaks. After placing clean paper underneath the engine, run the engine at medium speed until the oil is hot. Stop the engine and check for oil drippings on the paper. Trace the leak to its source and correct it. In many cases the leak is the sole cause of abnormal oil consumption. It's been estimated that a single drop of oil lost every fifty feet will amount to a full quart every 500 miles, an amount worth saving.

Greater oil consumption is normal if the oil used is too light or if the engine is run often at high speeds. A break-in period for new rings also requires additional oil.

High Ring Friction

In a newly rebuilt engine, poor performance is sometimes due to too much ring friction. Firm expander springs often press the rings too tightly against the cylinder walls. Engine power and gas economy drop conspicuously.

Test for excessive ring friction by holding the throttle open to an engine speed of 1000 rpm. Then turn off the ignition. An engine with proper tension will slow to stop and then roll back and forth momentarily. An engine with tight rings will stop suddenly without rolling.

Adjusting Valve Clearance

Improper valve clearance adjustment

results in loss of power and possible valve damage. Excessive clearance can be detected by noisy valves. Insufficient clearance causes valves to burn and possible backfiring through the carburetor.

When the engine is at operating temperature, remove the air cleaner and rocker cover. Turn the engine over by hand until the pushrod stops falling—the valve is fully closed at this point.

Basic valve-clearance adjustment for each cylinder is at the point where both valves are closed, TDC of the piston's compression stroke. Follow the firing order of the engine which is 1-3-4-2. Final adjustment of all valves is when the engine is at operating temperature and slowly idling. See Chapter 3 for details of valve adjustment.

Troubleshooting Engine Noises

If engine noises can be located and analyzed before the engine is disassembled, correcting the problem is much easier. Of course fine tuning is not possible until mechanical engine troubles are repaired. For locating noises, a piece of water hose of convenient length is a handy substitute for a stethoscope.

Valve Noises

Valve noise is a loud rhythmic clicking that varies directly with rpm, but occurs at half the beat of other engine noises because the camshaft rotates at half the engine speed.

Remove the valve covers to help locate noises better. Set engine rpm to the speed where the noise is most pronounced. If needed, hold end of piece of hose half an inch from tappets and listen to one valve at a time until the noisemaker is identified.

Sticky valves and tappets with excessive clearance have similar sounds although sticking-valve noises are normally intermittent. Check for excessive tappet clearance by inserting a feeler gauge between the noisy valve stem and its tappet. If the noise stops, reset the clearance. Remember, valves will burn if clearance is reduced below factory specifications. Valve sticking becomes pronounced when the engine idles after having been run hard. As the idling engine cools to its normal operating temperature the sticking-valve noise lessens. When a valve sticks, the lost compression from improper closing makes the engine idle roughly.

Warped and burnt valves also cause the engine to run irregularly, especially under low-speed load. They sometimes click but more often make hissing, wheezing sounds through the exhaust manifold (exhaust valve) or back fire (intake valve) through the carburetor.

Broken springs and bent valve stems don't close valves properly and are noisy as well.

Loose rocker arms and bent or worn pushrods transmit heavy rattling sounds.

Piston Noises

Generally, piston noises result from a piston slapping from side to side in its bore due to excessive clearance. However, if the piston noise is faint in a cold engine and disappears shortly after the engine reaches operating temperature, the condition might not be worth special attention.

Individual piston noises can be detected by shorting out one spark plug at a time while the engine is under partial load until the noise ceases. The piston makes no noise when its spark plug doesn't fire. A collapsed or badly worn piston makes a lowpitched, dull, metallic noise when the engine is under a load.

Broken rings or a cylinder ridge not removed when installing new rings will produce a steady, clicking, metallic noise at all engine speeds.

Loose wrist pins give a sharp metallic knock that is more noticeable when the engine is idling. Speeding up the engine to about 1500 rpm and then releasing the throttle is another way to detect the wrist pin knock.

Crankshaft Bearing Noises

Crankshaft noises can be grouped into main bearing noise, connecting rod noise, and crankshaft end-play noise.

A loose main bearing gives a heavy bumping noise when the engine is under load.

A loose connecting rod bearing has a steady rap after letting up slightly on the accelerator when car is driven about 50 mph. Shorting one spark plug at a time relieves pressure on each connecting rod bearing in turn and thereby deadens the noise of the defective bearing.

Excessive crankshaft end-play can be heard as a thud each time the clutch pedal is depressed. A rasping noise, when speeding and slowing the engine, indicates a loose fly wheel.

Detonation

Detonation, an explosion rather than a smooth burning of the fuel in a cylinder, is caused by an imbalance of compression, heat, fuel, valves, and timing. Detonation can be devastating to engine parts. Each of the following problems must be eliminated to prevent detonation.

A. Excessive cooling system temperature
B. Insufficient spark plug heat range
C. Over-advanced ignition timing
D. Too-low fuel octane rating
E. Lean carburetor fuel mixture
F. Stuck manifold heat control valve

With the ignition system checked, the vacuum and compression readings interpreted, and engine noises investigated, the mechanic should have a good indication of any mechanical defects in the engine. These malfunctions should be corrected before attempting to tune the engine. Detailed overhaul procedures for the ignition system and engine mechanical parts are provided in later chapters.

Cleaning Fuel System

A final pre-tune-up step involves cleaning the carburetors, fuel filters and, if necessary, lines and tank.

Many fuel system problems result from accumulation of water, dirt, and gummy residues in the tank, lines, and pump. Other problems are caused by restricted tank ventilation, leaky lines and connections, and worn out moving parts. These troubles, when identified before disassembly, can be eliminated efficiently.

Ideally, the carburetor should be taken apart, cleaned thoroughly, and reassembled with new gasketing and other non-metal parts. If complete disassembly is not feasible, it is recommended that carburetor jets be removed from time to time and blown through with compressed air. Wash carburetor housing with gasoline (engine COLD) to remove dirt. Remove only one jet at a time for cleaning to prevent a mistake on replacement. (NOTE: the jets should not be cleaned with a sharp or abrasive object that might cause deformation of the close factory calibration.)

Checking Fuel-Air Mixtures

Poor engine performance can be caused by air-fuel mixtures that are either too rich or too lean. Both maladjustments are harmful to the engine. A lean mixture at high speeds overheats the combustion chambers to the point where valves might burn. A rich mixture washes lubricating oil from the cylinders, resulting in scuffed rings and scored cylinder walls.

Rub paper or cloth around the inside of the exhaust pipe, checking for carbon deposits. A rich mixture leaves a black residue.

Choke off the carburetor(s) while the warmed engine is running at 1500 rpm. (The palm of the hand can be used to restrict incoming air.) By reducing the air flow, the air-fuel mixture is normally enriched and the engine speeds up somewhat. If it doesn't speed up at all, the mixture adjustment is *too rich;* if it speeds up drastically, the mixture adjustment is *too lean.*

When a carburetor has a lean mixture, the engine pauses and then accelerates poorly with apparent sponginess (there might be backfiring). If a weak fuel pump or restricted gas line is the cause of the lean mixture, the engine runs out of fuel at higher engine speeds.

Rich mixture can be caused by high fuel pressure forcing the needle valve from its seat. The carburetor floods and performance breaks down.

A malfunctioning carburetor cannot be tuned, so should be overhauled. Detailed procedures are in Chapter 3.

Cleaning Fuel Filters

Loosen the cover hex bolt and remove the screen from the mechanical fuel pump. Wash screen and cover in solvent and blow dry with air. Replace gasket if necessary and reinstall screen, cover and bolt. Then start engine and check for leaks.

Cleaning Air Filters

To clean the dry paper filter, remove and tap lightly to loosen dirt, or blow out with compressed air. Restricted filters will adversely affect engine performance. If too dirty, replace the element.

Oil-wetted, metal-mesh filters can be washed in solvent. Blow out with compressed air or let dry in the open. Re-oil lightly prior to installation.

Cleaning Carburetor Parts

All carburetors have numerous small passages that can be fouled by carbon and gummy deposits. Metal parts should

Piston damaged by inaudible detonation and pre-ignition at high speeds.

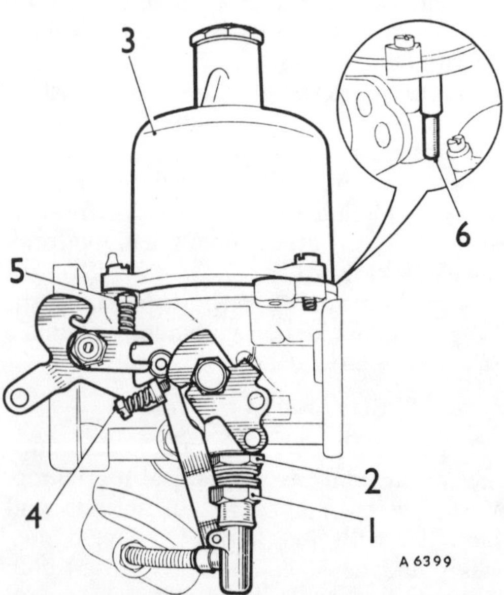

The Type HS Carburetor

1. Jet adjusting nut
2. Jet locking nut
3. Piston/suction chamber
4. Fast-idle adjusting screw
5. Throttle adjusting screw
6. Piston lifting pin

Tuning Single Carburetors

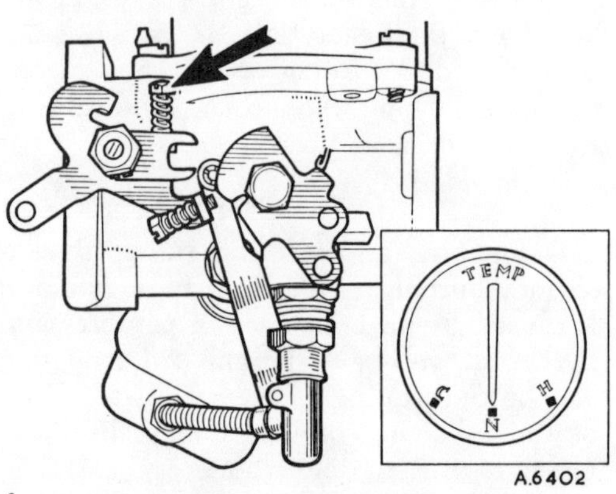

1.

A. Warm engine up to normal temperature.
B. Switch off engine.
C. Unscrew the throttle adjusting screw until it is just clear of its stop and the throttle is closed.
D. Set throttle adjusting screw 1½ turns open.

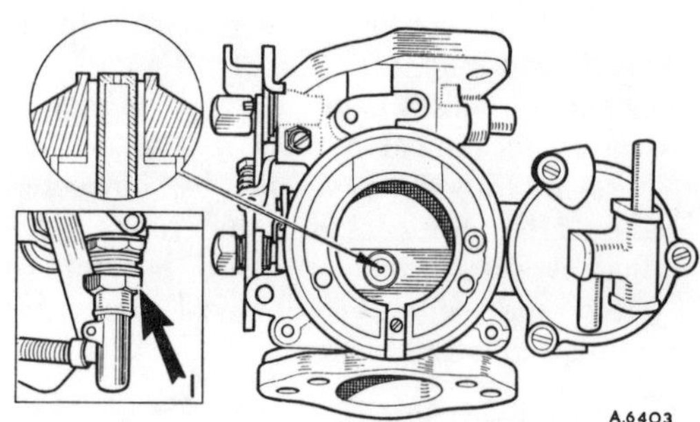

2.

A. Mark for reassembly and remove piston/suction chamber unit.
B. Disconnect mixture control wire.
C. Screw the jet adjusting nut (1) until the jet is flush with the bridge of the carburetor or fully up if this position cannot be obtained.

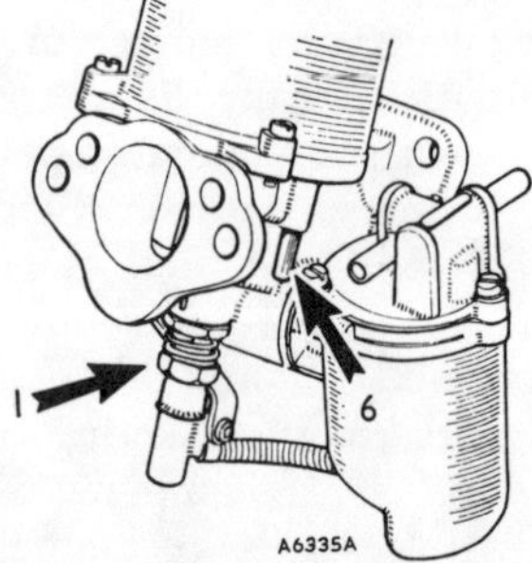

3.

A. Replace the piston/suction chamber unit as marked.
B. Check that the piston falls freely onto the bridge when the lifting pin (6) is released. If not, see items 15, 16 and 17.
C. Turn down the jet adjusting nut (1) two complete turns.

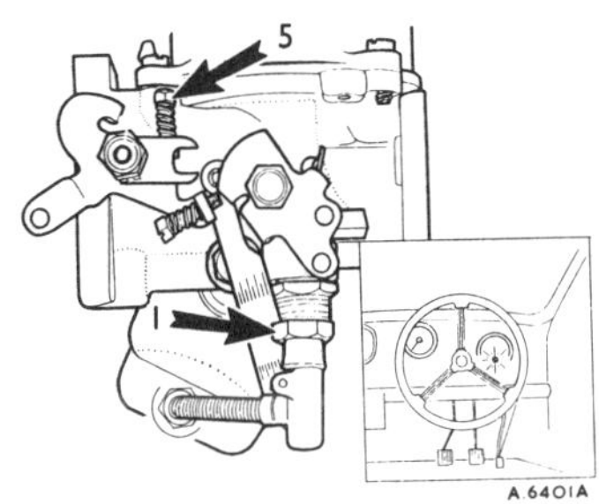

4.

A. Restart the engine and adjust the throttle adjusting screw (5) to give desired idling as indicated by the glow of the ignition warning light.

B. Turn the jet adjusting nut (1) up to weaken or down to richen until the fastest idling speed consistent with even running is obtained.

C. Readjust the throttle adjusting screw (5) to give correct idling if necessary.

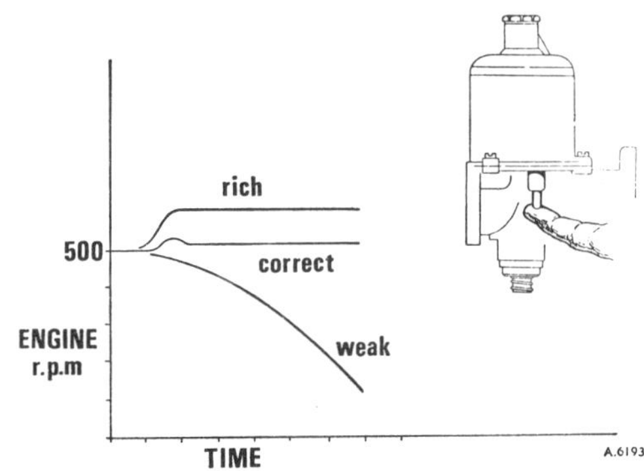

6.

A. Check for correct mixture by gently pushing the lifting pin up about 1/32 in. (.8 mm.) after free movement has been taken up.

B. The graph illustrates the effect on engine rpm when the lifting pin raises the piston, indicating the mixture strength.
Rich mixture: rpm increases considerably.
Correct mixture: rpm increases very slightly.
Weak mixture: rpm immediately decreases.

C. Readjust the mixture strength if necessary.

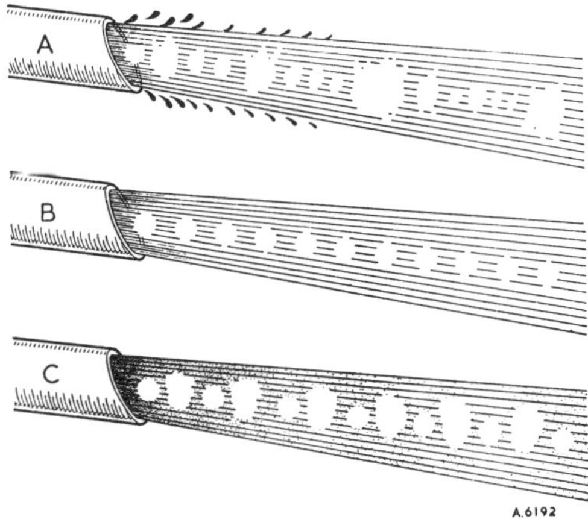

5.

The effect of mixture strength on exhaust smoke.

A. Too weak: irregular note, splashy misfire and colorless.

B. Correct: regular and even note.

C. Too rich: regular or rhythmical, blackish.

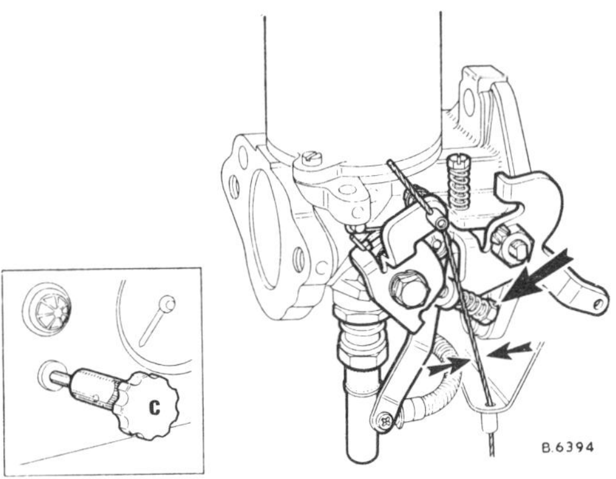

7.

A. Reconnect the mixture control wire with about 1/16 in. (1.6 mm.) free movement before it starts to pull on the jet lever.

B. Pull the mixture control knob until the linkage is about to move the carburetor jet and adjust the fast-idle screw to give an engine speed of about 1,000 rpm when hot.

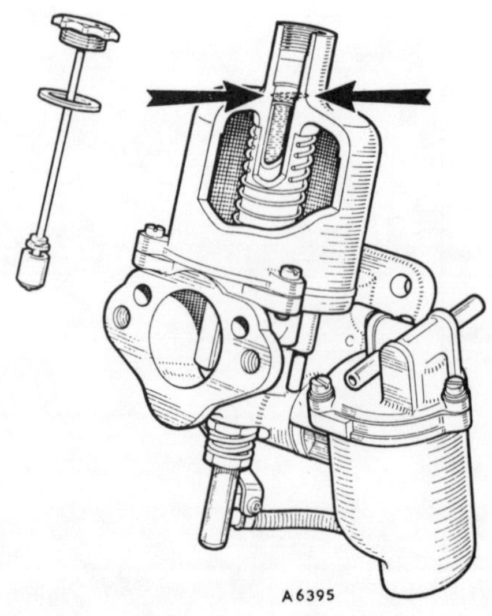

8.

Finally top up the piston damper with the recommended engine oil until the level is ½ in. (13 mm.) above the top of the hollow piston rod.

Note: On dust-proofed carburetors, identified by a transverse hole drilled in the neck of the suction chambers and no vent hole in the damper cap, the oil level should be ½ in. (13 mm.) below the top of the hollow piston rod.

Tuning Multi-Carburetors

Remove the air cleaners and carry out item 1 as for single on all carburetors; then:

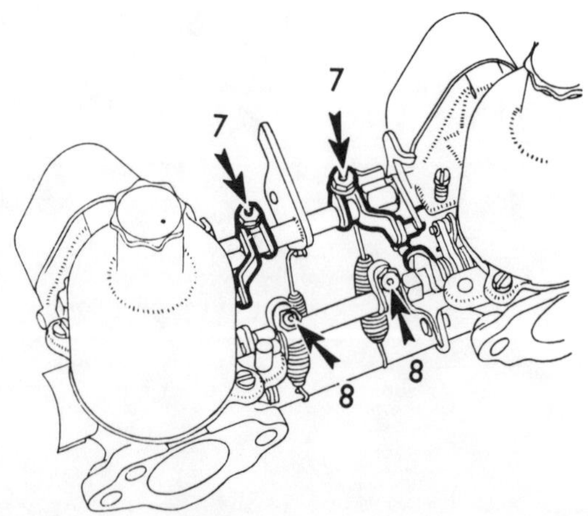

9.

A. Slacken both of the clamping bolts (7) on the throttle spindle interconnections.

B. Disconnect the jet control interconnection by slackening the clamping bolts (8).

C. Carry out items 2 and 3 as for single carburetors, then additionally:

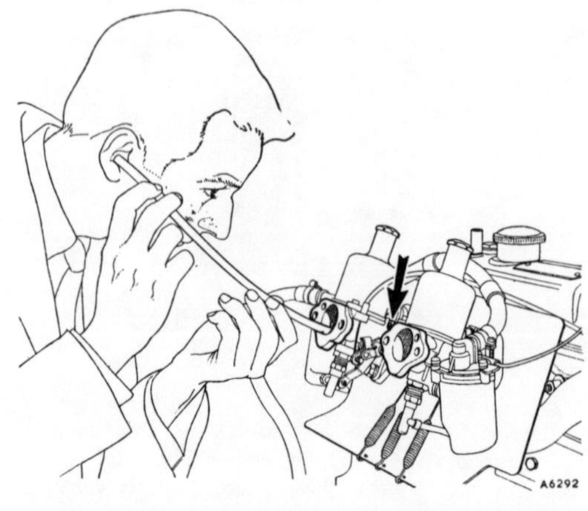

10.

A. Restart the engine and adjust the throttle adjusting screws on each carburetor to give the desired idling speed as indicated by the glow of the ignition warning light.

B. Compare the intensity of the intake "hiss" on all carburetors and alter the throttle adjusting screws until the "hiss" is the same.

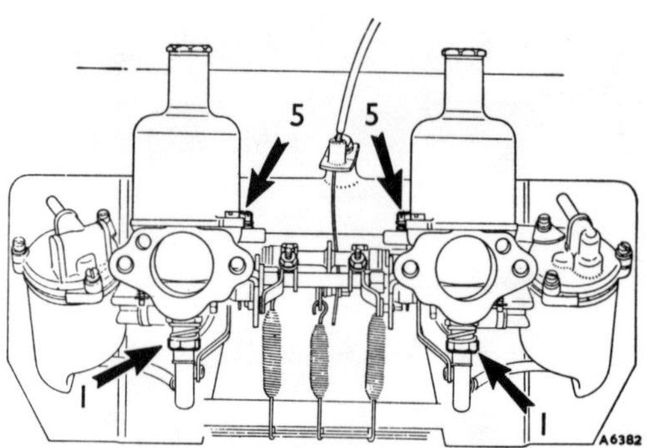

11.

A. Turn the jet adjusting nuts (1) on all carburetors up to weaken or down to richen by the same amount until the fastest idling speed consistent with even running is obtained.

B. Readjust the throttle adjusting screws (5) to give correct idling if necessary.

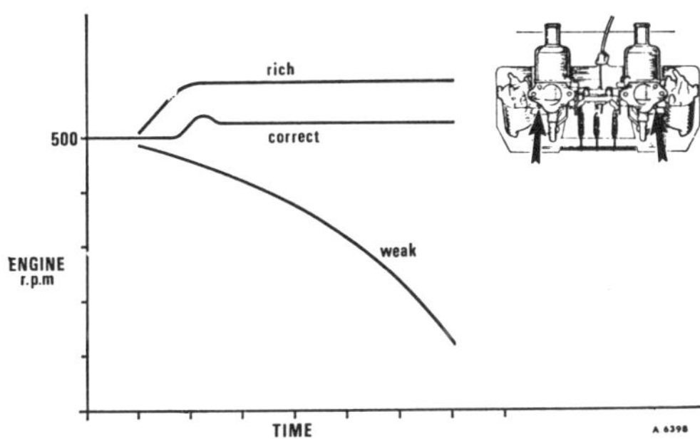

12.

A. Check for correct mixture by gently pushing the lifting pin of the front carburetor up 1/32 in. (. 8mm.) after free movement has been taken up. The graph illustrates the possible effect on engine rpm. Readjust the mixture strength if necessary.

B. Repeat the operation on the other carburetors and after adjustment recheck since they are all interdependent.

C. Item 5 shows the correct type of exhaust smoke.

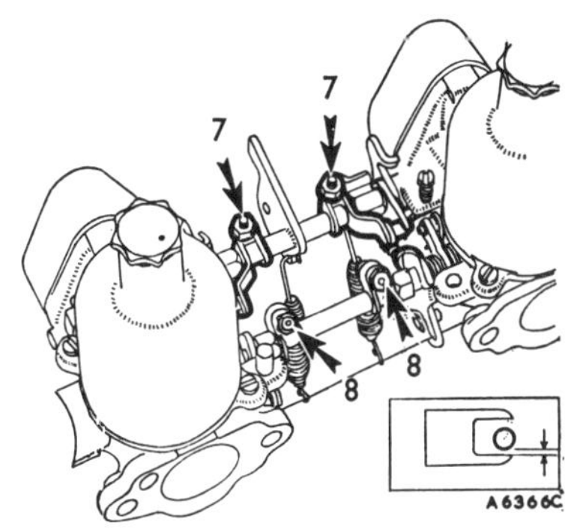

13.

A. Set the throttle interconnection clamping levers (7) so that the link pin is .006 in. (.15 mm.) away from the lower edge of the fork (see inset). Tighten the clamp bolts.

B. With both jet levers at their lowest position, set the jet interconnection lever clamp bolts (8) so that both jets begin to move simultaneously.

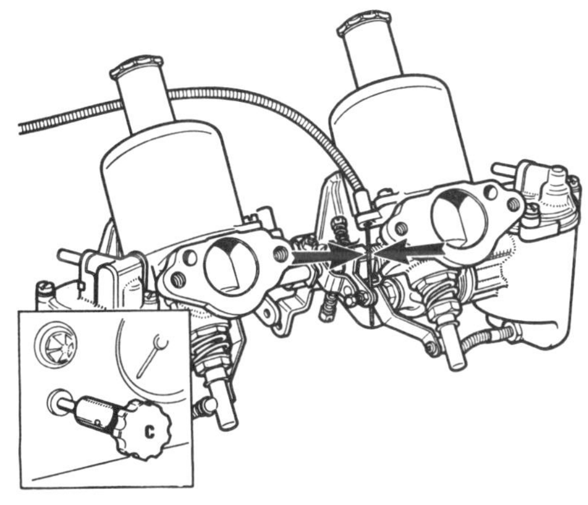

14.

A. Reconnect the mixture control wire with about 1/16 in. (1.6 mm.) free movement before it starts to pull on the jet levers.

B. Pull the mixture control knob until the linkage is about to move the carburetor jets, and adjust the fast idle screws, comparing the intensity of the air intake "hiss" to give an an engine speed of about 1,000 rpm when hot.

C. Refit the air cleaners.

Adjusting and Servicing Jet Centering

15.

The piston should fall freely onto the carburetor bridge with a click when the lifting pin is released with the jet in the fully up position. If it will do this only with the jet lowered, then the jet unit requires re-centering. This is done as follows:

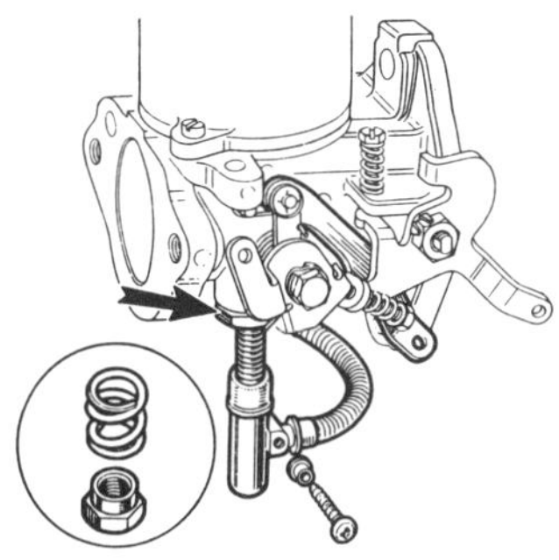

16.

A. Remove the jet head screw to release the control linkage.

B. Withdraw the jet, disconnecting the fuel feed pipe union in the float-chamber, and removing the rubber sealing washer. Remove the jet locking spring and adjusting nut.

C. Replace the jet and insert the fuel feed pipe connection into the float-chamber.

D. Slacken the jet locking nut until the assembly is free to rotate.

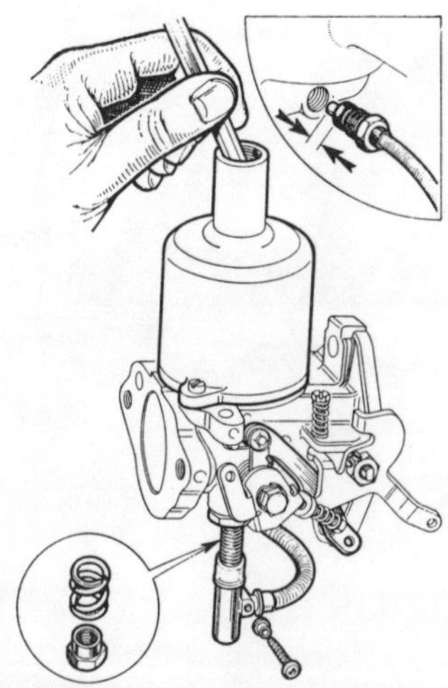

17.

A. Remove the piston damper and apply pressure to the top of the piston rod with a pencil.

B. Tighten the jet locking nut keeping the jet hard up against the jet bearing.

C. Finally check again as in item 15.

D. Re-fit the jet locking spring and adjusting nut. Before replacing the fuel feed pipe in the float-chamber, fit the rubber sealing washer over the end of the plastic pipe so that at least 3/16 in. (4.8 mm.) of pipe protrudes (see inset). Reassemble the controls.

E. Refill the piston dampers with the recommended engine oil (see item 8).

Cleaning

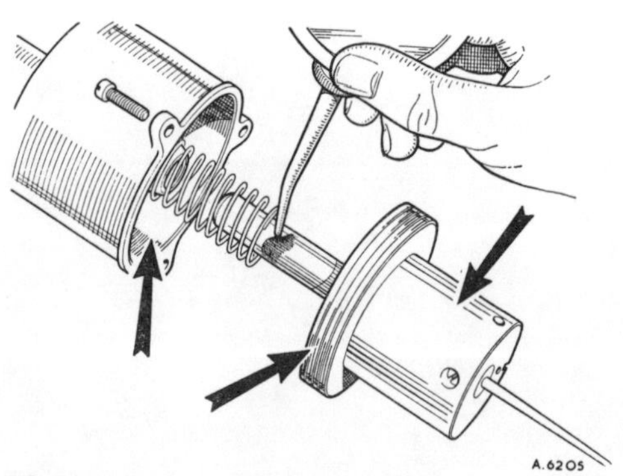

18.

A. At the recommended intervals, mark for re-assembly and carefully remove the piston/suction chamber unit.

B. Using an oil-moistened cloth, clean the inside bore of the suction chamber and the two diameters of the piston.

C. Lightly oil the piston rod only and reassemble as marked.

D. Refill piston damper (see item 8).

Float-Chamber Fuel Level

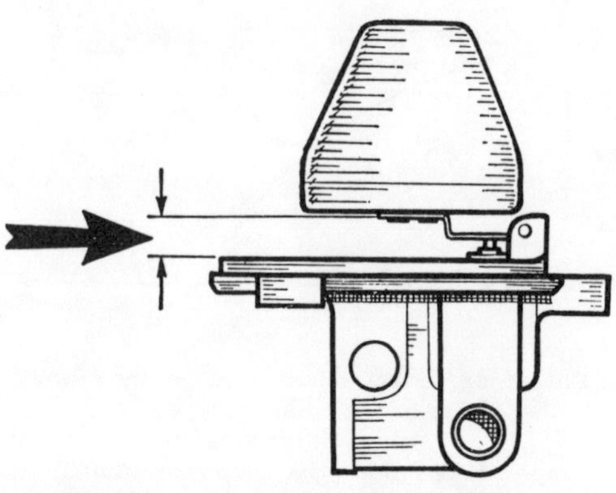

19.

A. Remove and invert the float-chamber lid.

B. With the needle valve held in the shut-off position by the weight of the float only, there should be a 1/8 to 3/16 in. (3.2 to 4.8 mm.) gap between the float lever and the rim of the float-chamber lid.

C. The float may be set by bending at the crank.

Needle Size and Position

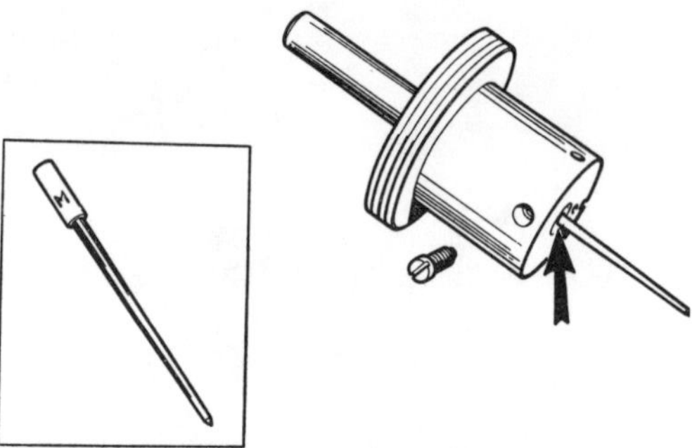

20.

A. The needle size is determined during engine development and will provide the correct mixture strength unless extremes of temperature, humidity, or altitude are encountered. At altitudes exceeding 6,000 ft. (1830 m.) a weaker needle will be necessary. A diferent needle may also be necessary if any alteration to the standard specification of the exhaust system, air cleaner, camshaft, or compression ratio is made.

B. To check that the correct needle is fitted: mark for reassembly and remove the piston/suction chamber unit.

C. Slacken the needle clamping screw, extract the needle, and check its identifying mark against the recommendation.

D. Replace the correct needle and lock it in position so that the shoulder on the shank is flush with the piston base.

E. Reassemble the piston/suction chamber unit as marked.

Summary

Symptom	*Cause*	*Remedy*	*Item No.*
Erratic running Stalling at idling Lack of power High fuel consumption	Sticking piston: Dirty piston and suction chamber	Clean	18
	Jet out of centre	Re-centre	15, 16, and 17
	Bent needle	Fit new	20
Hesitation at pick-up	Low damper oil level	Top up	8
	Incorrect oil grade (too thin)	Replace with correct grade	8
Fuel leak from float-chamber/feed pipe union	Rubber sealing washer displaced or damaged	Renew	17
Float-chamber flooding	Dirty or worn float-chamber needle valve (dirty fuel)	Clean or renew valve (flush system)	
	Punctured float	Fit new	
	Incorrect fuel level	Check and reset level	19

be soaked in carburetor solvent until thoroughly clean. However, the solvent will weaken or destroy cork, plastic and leather components. These parts should be wiped with a clean, lint-free cloth.

While the carburetor is disassembled, check the bowl cover with a straight edge for warped surfaces.

The needle valves and seats should be closely inspected for wear and damage. Replace these parts when imperfect because their performance affects engine tuning most critically.

After cleaning the parts, blow air through the high and low speed jets to ensure that all passages are clear.

Reassemble the carburetor, using new gaskets and other non-metal parts.

Lubricating Carburetor Linkage

Lubricate all pivot points with 1–2 drops of engine oil while moving throttle controls. Lubricate accelerator pump rods. Disconnect all ball joints, fill cups with grease, reconnect. Move linkage back and forth to check for proper functioning.

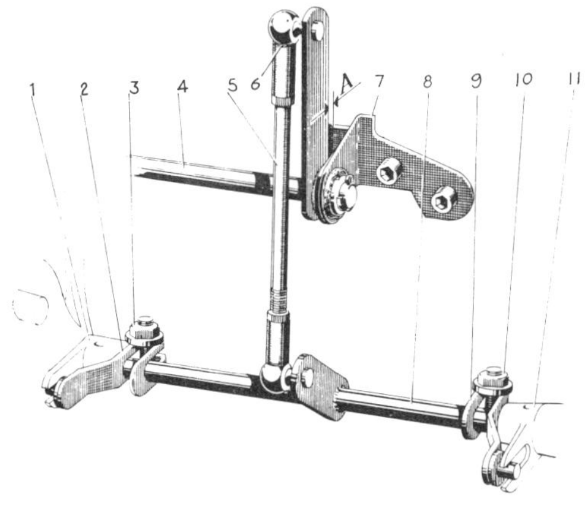

1. Lever on throttle spindle
2. Lever on intermediate spindle
3. Locknut
4. Control shaft
5. Link rod
6. Lock wire
7. Bracket
8. Intermediate shaft
9. Lever on intermediate shaft
10. Locknut
11. Lever on throttle spindle

Throttle rod linkage—B20B engine with SU-HS6 carburetors.

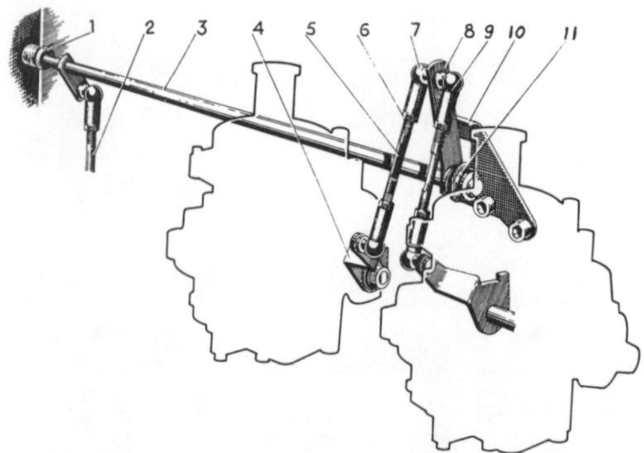

1. Bushing
2. Link rod for pedal
3. Control shaft
4. Lever
5. Link rod
6. Locknut
7. Ball joint
8. Lever
9. Lock wire
10. Bracket
11. Rubber mounting

Throttle rod linkage—B20B engine with Zenith-Stromberg 175 CD-2SE carburetors.

Adjusting the Carburetor

Of utmost importance in tuning is the reminder that carburetors can only be adjusted satisfactorily when the engine is in good condition and the timing is perfect. (Before adjusting fuel mixture on the carburetor, check the accelerator pump discharge at pump nozzles.)

Synchronizing Twin Carburetors

First warm up the engine, remove air cleaner, disconnect throttle linkage, and adjust for equal idling on the carburetors at a higher idling speed of 1000 to 1200 rpm.

If a carburetor synchronizing gauge is available, adjust it on one carburetor throat to a piston height near the middle of the scale. Switch the test gauge to the other carburetor and, if necessary, reset the air-adjustment screw of that carb until the synchronizing gauge piston returns to the middle position. NOTE: *do not reset the gauge level*

1968 and later cars have an intake manifold which heats the intake mixture by circulating it through baffles heated by the exhaust gases in the exhaust manifold. In addition to heating the mixture, the manifold also acts as a plenum chamber, and reduces the necessity of close synchronization of the carburetors.

Idle Adjustment—Zenith Stromberg 175-CD-2S/2SE

The 175-CD-2S/2SE carburetor contains a single jet with a tapered needle that is operated by an air valve and carburetor vacuum. There is no special idling system. The fuel air mixture is set at idling speed by the single adjusting screw at the bottom of the carburetor and applies to the entire speed range. There is no choke as such. Rather, a disc-like cold starting device, when actuated, depresses the jet, giving a richer mixture. Therefore, there are two adjustments, one for the proper fuel-air mixture and the fast idle stop screw for proper idling speed. To make these adjustments, remove the air cleaner and proceed as follows:

1. Press the air valve down, and screw in the fuel-air mixture adjusting screw at the bottom of the carburetor until the jet just touches the valve. Then unscrew the adjusting screw 1½ turns.
2. Run the engine until it is warm.
3. Adjust the fast idle stop screw for an idle speed of about 600 rpm.

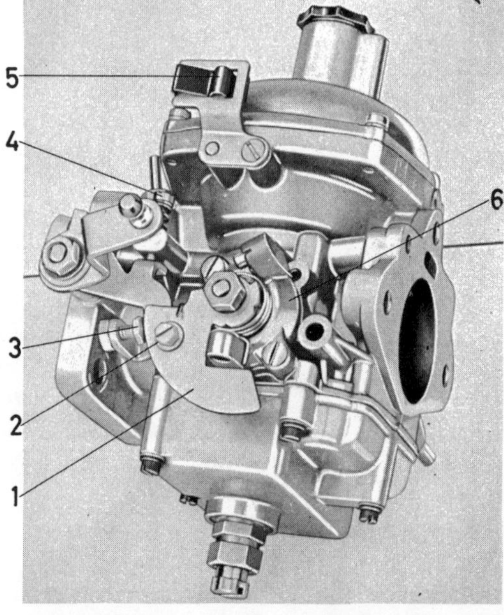

1. Choke cam
2. Choke control connection
3. Fast-idle stop screw
4. Throttle stop screw
5. Attaching sleeve for choke control
6. Cold start device

Zenith-Stromberg 175-CD-2S horizontal carburetor

4. Screw in the fuel mixture adjusting screw until the engine starts to run unevenly. Then slowly turn the screw in the opposite direction until the engine again starts to run unevenly. Finally turn the screw back to a point somewhere between these two positions.

5. Adjust the fast idle stop screw until it barely touches the choke cam at a point about one-half inch from the upper part of the cam when it is turned upwards. (In extremely cold weather, adjust the screw so that it touches the choke cam when the choke control is pushed in fully).

Idle Adjustment—Zenith 36VN

The down-draft Zenith 36VN has a hand regulated choke, fixed main and idling jets and an acceleration pump. Fuel air mixture at idling speed is controlled by an adjustment screw.

Adjust the carburetor for engine idling by first warming up the engine. At idling speed, screw in the fuel-air mixture idling adjustment until the engine speeds up. Then slowly unscrew the adjustment until the engine speeds up. Then slowly unscrew the adjustment until the engine idles slowly but evenly. Finally, screw in the adjustment until the engine just runs smoothly.

Idle and Choke Adjustment—SU-HS6

When starting with a cold engine the fuel-air mixture is enriched by a lowering of the jets through manual operation of the choke on the instrument panel. In addition, the fast idling screw is moved somewhat by a cam on the choke lever, opening the throttle plate slightly.

Obtain the proper fuel-air mixture and idling adjustment as follows after warming engine:

1. Adjust both carburetors at the same time. First, screw in the fuel-air mixture adjusting nut at the bottom of each carburetor to its upper position, and then back it off 1½ turns.

2. Adjust the idle screw on each carb equally and to obtain an engine idling speed of about 600 rpm. Turn the screws so that the intake sounds of the carbs are equal strength.

3. Without touching the idle screw, adjust the fuel-air mixture nut at the bottom of each carb one at a time, by first turning slowly downwards (richer mixture) and then upwards (leaner mixture) until the engine runs smoothly. The best position is reached when the highest engine speed is obtained without altering the idle adjusting screw.

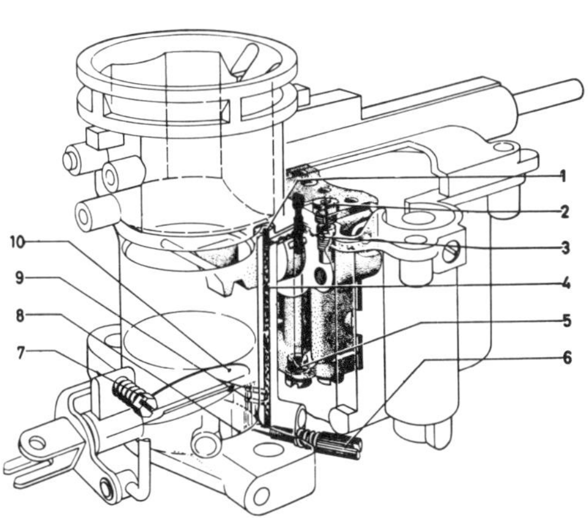

1. Air hole
2. Idling air jet
3. Idling jet
4. Idling channel
5. Main jet
6. Fuel-air mixture idling adjustment
7. Fast-idle stop screw
8. Venturi
9. Transition holes
10. Throttle flap

Zenith 36VN down-draught carburetor.

1. Attachment for choke control outer casing
2. Idle adjusting screw
3. Fast idle adjusting screw
4. Lever
5. Choke control locking screw
6. Locknut
7. Fuel-air mixture adjusting nut
8. Jet

Type S.U. carburetor.

4. Adjusting equally on both carburetors, adjust the idle screws for proper idling speed.

5. Check that the fuel-air mixture is correct, first in one carburetor then in the other by lifting the piston, using the pin beside the air intake.

The engine should run with about the same unevenness in both cases, and the speed should fall off to about 450 or 500 rpm. If the engine stalls when one of the carb pistons is lifted, the mixture in the other carb is too lean. If engine speed increases, the mixture in the other carb is too rich.

The choke control and fast idling adjustments are made as follows, keeping in mind that adjustments must always be made so that both carburetors are affected to exactly the same extent by the control:

1. Pull out choke control on the instrument panel about ⅝″.

2. Loosen the locking screw for the choke control cable. Lift the lever enough to let the jet start to go down.

3. Adjust the fast idle screw so that it just touches the fast idle cam on the lever when the jet starts to go down as described in Step 3. Tighten the control cable locking screw.

4. Check that both carburetors are operated to the same extent by pulling the choke control cable and watching the jets go down. Adjust setting if jets do not go down equally.

1. Hydraulic chamber
2. Suction chamber
3. Designation plate
4. Fuel line connection
5. Hose connection to air cleaner (float chamber vent)
6. Float chamber
7. Fuel line from float chamber to jet
8. Lever
9. By-pass valve
10. Primary throttle
11. Connection flange

SU-HS6 Carburetor, left side.

Idle and Choke Adjustment (B14A and B16B Engines)

B14A engines employ twin horizontal Type SU-H2 carburetors, while B16B enines are equipped with twin horizontal SU-H4 types. Except for slight variations in float and choking arrangements, these carburetors are similar to the SU-HS6 twin carburetors and adjustment can be carried out as previously described for the B18B/D engines.

Exhaust Emission Control

Volvo has reduced the engine emissions by designing the engines to run very effi-

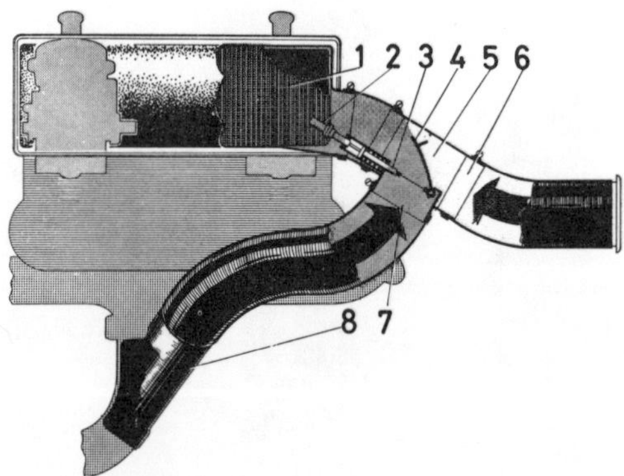

1. Air cleaner
2. Thermostat
3. Flap control
4. Flap
5. Flap housing
6. Cold air intake
7. Warm air intake
8. Heater plate on exhaust manifold

Emission control air preheater system.

ciently. Carburetor intake air is kept at a constant temperature by a thermostatic valve which mixes cold outside air and warm air heated by the exhaust manifold. This allows the carburetors to be set at a very efficient mixture, and to always hold the mixture, regardless of outside air temperature.

The fuel-air mixture is heated in the intake manifold in a preheating chamber. The exhaust manifold heats baffles in the intake manifold which heats the fuel-air mixture as it passes around the baffles.

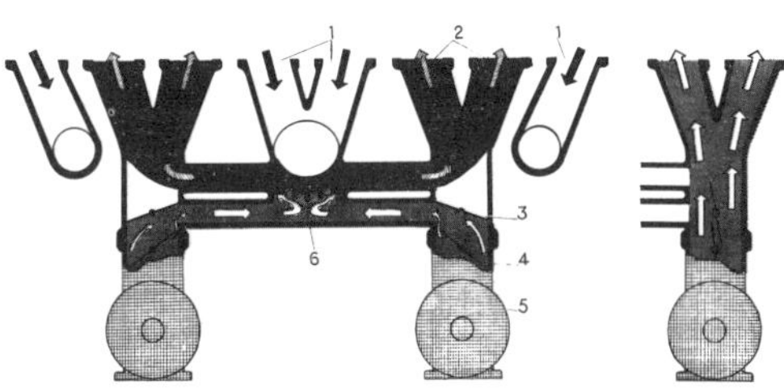

1. Exhaust manifold
2. Intake manifold
3. Secondary throttle
4. Primary throttle
5. Carburetor
6. Preheating Chamber

Emission control manifold heating system—B20B engine.

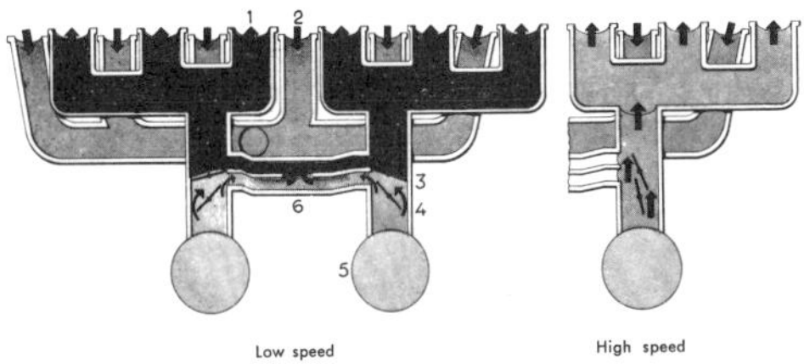

1. Intake manifold
2. Exhaust manifold
3. Secondary throttle
4. Primary throttle
5. Carburetor
6. Preheating chamber

Emission control manifold heating system—B30 engine.

By keeping temperatures of the air and fuel-air mixture constant, the engine can be tuned to run very efficiently, without any compensation for changes in air temperature.

The distributor is equipped with a vacuum advance unit, which gives a greater range of ignition timing than before. At idle and during deceleration, the timing is retarded considerably to reduce the quantity of unburned gases, but advances normally during acceleration and high speed running.

Clutch Troubleshooting

Clutch slippage, chatter, and grabbing are most noticeable when accelerating from a standstill in first or reverse gears.

Dragging of the clutch is obvious when shifting between gears, especially into and out of reverse.

DRAGGING—fails to release completely

a. Excessive linkage free play
b. Sticking or faulty pilot bearing
c. Damaged clutch plates (pressure and/or driven)
d. Release yoke off pivot ball-stud
e. Driven-plate hub binding on main drive gear spline

SLIPPING—does not firmly engage

a. Insufficient linkage free play
b. Oil-soaked driven disc (correct oil leak before installing new assembly)
c. Worn or damaged driven disc
d. Warped pressure plate or flywheel
e. Weak diaphragm spring (replace cover assembly)
f. Driven plate not seated (make 20–50 normal starts)
g. Driven plate overheated (check lash after cooled)

GRABBING-CHATTER—intermittent seizing and slipping

a. Oil spotted, burned or glazed facings
b. Worn splines on main drive gear or clutch disc
c. Loose engine or drive train mountings
d. Warped pressure plate, clutch disc or flywheel
e. Burned or smeared resin on flywheel or pressure plate (sand

smooth if superficial, replace if burned or heat-checked

RATTLING—transmission click

a. Release yoke and leave loose on pivot ball-stud or in bearing groove (replace if necessary)
b. Oil in driven-disc damper (replace driven-disc
c. Driven-disc damper spring failure (replace driven-disc)

THROW-OUT BEARING NOISE—clutch fully engaged

a. Improper linkage adjustment
b. Throw-out bearing binding on transmission bearing retainer (clean, lubricate, check for burrs, nicks)
c. Insufficient tension between release yoke and pivot ball-stud (yoke improperly installed and/or linkage spring weak)

TIGHT PEDAL—when depressed or returns sluggishly

a. Bind in linkage (lubricate and free up)
b. Weak pressure plate spring
c. Weak linkage spring
d. Driven disc worn

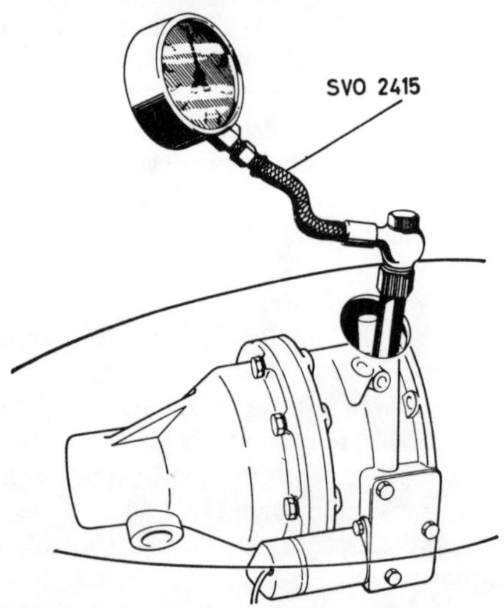

Checking overdrive oil pressure through access hole.

Transmission Troubleshooting

NOISE—in forward speeds

a. Low lubricant level or incorrect lubricant
b. Transmission misaligned or loose
c. Mainshaft bearing or front main bearing worn or damaged
d. Countergear or bearings worn or damaged
e. Main drive gear or synchronizers worn or damaged

NOISE—in reverse

a. Reverse sliding gear or shaft, worn or damaged

HARD SHIFTING

a. Clutch improperly adjusted
b. Shift shafts or forks worn
c. Incorrect lubricant
d. Synchronizers worn or broken

JUMPING OUT OF GEAR

a. Partial engagement of gear
b. Transmission misaligned or loose
c. Worn pilot bearing
d. End play in main drive gear (bearing retainer loose or broken, loose or worn bearings on main drive gear and mainshaft)
e. Worn clutch teeth on main drive gear and/or on synchronizer sleeve
f. Worn or broken blocking rings
g. Bent mainshaft

STICKING IN GEAR

a. Clutch not released fully
b. Low lubricant level or incorrect lubrication
c. Defective (tight) main drive gear pilot bearing
d. Frozen blocking ring on main drive gear cone
e. Burred or battered teeth on synchronizer sleeve and/or main drive gear

Overdrive Troubleshooting

If faulty operation should be experienced with the transmission overdrive it may be due to a clogged oil strainer, improper overdrive pump pressure or defective control valve performance.

The following tests should help locate the trouble: The oil strainer should be cleaned at every oil change. Drain oil by removing plug marked "drain" under the oil strainer. Remove cover. Take out oil strainer and magnetic washers, clean with gasoline and blow dry with compressed air. Check that oil strainer gasket is in good condition, insert in position with steel-covered side toward housing. Install oil strainer, washers, new cover gasket and cover.

Oil Pressure Check

Disengage overdrive to remove residual pressure. Remove plug over control valve and connect gauge SVO 2415. Allow spring, tappet and ball to remain in position. Start engine and drive car. At a speed of 31-37 mph on overdrive, the gauge should show a reading of 500-570 lbs./sq. in (35–40 kg/cm²). If reading is low, first change spring and relief valve plunger. Then, if necessary, place washers under spring. (.004″ alters pressure about 14.22 lbs/sq in). Trouble can also be due to worn pump parts.

Checking Oil Pump

Switch out overdrive to remove any residual oil pressure. Jack up vehicle and place blocks under front and rear axles. Remove drain plug and drain oil into a container. Remove plug under oil pump and take out the spring and ball. Remove valve seating with key SVO 2419. Clean and inspect parts. Check with a piece of wire or something similar held against the pump plunger that the pump works when the output shaft is rotated. (Turn engine over a few times with overdrive switched in and ignition coil disconnected.) The pump plunger stroke should be .157″ (4 mm). If it is shorter, the pump must be removed and the trouble ascertained.

Remove pump by removing bolt which holds pump. Attach puller SVO 2418 into the place of the valve seating and pull out pump. Disassemble pump and check parts. Assemble in reverse order.

Checking Control Valve

Jack up vehicle and place blocks under front and rear axles. Remove cover from over control valve arm. Switch in overdrive (with engine stopped and shift lever in 4th speed). If control valve is properly adjusted, it should be possible to pass a 3⁄16″ diameter pin through the hole in the arm and into the housing. If not, adjust until correct position is obtained.

Check current through solenoid with overdrive in. Current should be about one ampere max. If current is 10-12 amp or higher, the control solenoid does not go in far enough to cut off the control current. Determine reason and adjust. Otherwise solenoid will be damaged.

Cleaning Control Valve

Remove plug over control valve as well as spring, tappet, ball and valve rod. Lift ball with loop of wire and valve rod with a pointed wood probe pushed into opening. Clean parts. Clean valve rod with 3.1 mm drill and valve hole with a 1.1 mm drill. Assemble parts in reverse order to above.

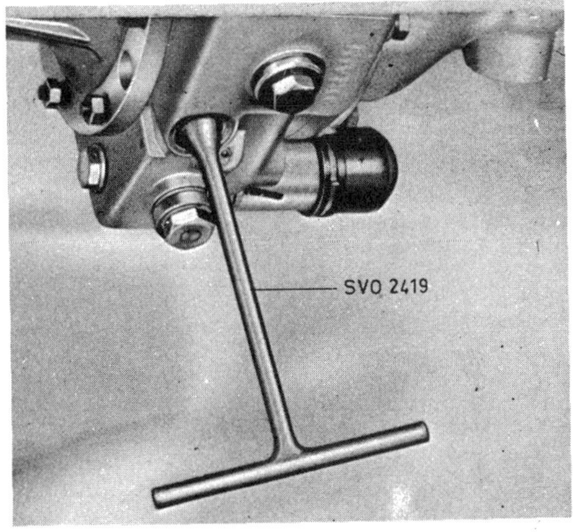

Removing overdrive oil pump valve seat.

Drive Shaft Troubleshooting

Defects in the drive shaft or drive shaft components are usually evidenced by vibration, thumping or clicking sounds. Vibration shows up as a growling noise which becomes louder as the speed increases and may be due to wear, a bent drive shaft, insufficient lubrication or improper assembly. No attempt should be made to repair a bent or damaged drive shaft. A new one should be installed as described in Chapter Eight. Worn universal joints usually cause a loud clicking sound if the car is driven slowly and speed is accelerated and decelerated. Replacement of universal joints and other parts are described also in Chapter Eight.

Front End Troubleshooting

When servicing steering and front suspension assemblies, it is advisable to check every front end part because all of the assemblies are so closely interrelated.

First, check the front end for worn or loose-fitting parts. Repair or replace what is faulty. Second, inspect and adjust the steering gear assembly. Third, set the front end alignment. And last, balance the wheels.

To detect front-end troubles quickly, follow these simple procedures:

1. With the front end jacked up, shake both wheels simultaneously to detect any looseness between them. Tie-rod and steering linkage joints sometimes loosen under severe road stresses. Check weaknesses further by oscillating and prying against members connected to these joints.
2. Check out wheel suspension joints by having each wheel shaken up and down while the steering knuckle and control arm joints are observed for play.
3. Spin the wheels rapidly to test for deteriorated bearings. Listen for bearing noise and touch the bumper to feel vibration that rough bearings create.
4. Rig a piece of chalk so it just clears the wheel rim and rotate the wheel to test for wheel runout. The chalk will mark misaligned, protruding rim areas. Repeat test on inside rim. Wheel should be straightened if runout exceeds ⅛ inch.

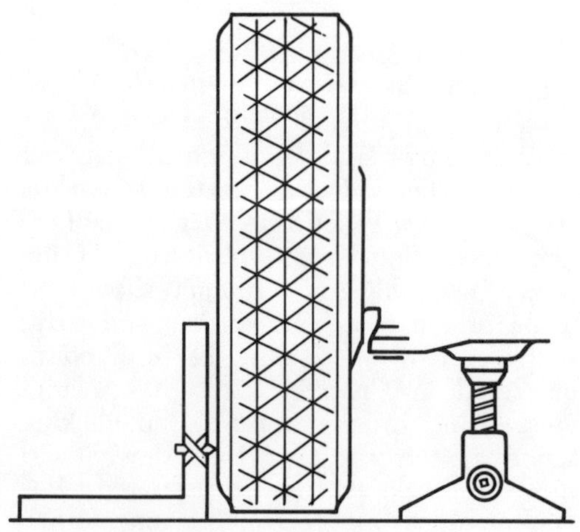

Testing for front wheel runout.

5. Lower front end to ground and rebound fenders to check for deteriorated shock absorbers.
6. Check pre-owned cars for possible front end damage by measuring and comparing the wheelbase on both sides. Measure carefully from common points such as from the rear of the front-wheel rim to the rear of the back-wheel rim. If one side has a shorter or longer wheelbase than is listed in specifications, compare several measurements on both sides between various points until the dislocated part is found.

Diagonal measurements from right front to left rear wheels and from left front to right rear wheels will uncover a distorted chassis (if wheelbase measurements are equal). A twisted chassis will alter tracking and make front end alignment difficult if not impossible.

Vehicle Wandering

Vehicle wandering requires constant steering wheel correction, is annoying and also dangerous. It may be caused by incorrect caster or toe-in, too low tire pressure, excessive or insufficient play in the steering mechanism, worn or stiff steering rod ball joints, stiff control arm system, excessive play in rear end suspension.

Pulling to One Side

Check for uneven tire pressure, weak or uneven front springs, stiff wheel bearing, faulty wheel alignment, dragging brake, bent steering rod, or incorrect camber.

Hard Steering

Caused by too-low tire pressure, insufficiently lubricated steering gears or front end, excessive caster, damaged bearing in gear housing or steering column, damaged thrust bearing in steering knuckles, damaged front axle member or body.

Shimmy

Look for bent, misaligned or unbalanced wheels, worn or warped brake drum, too-low tire pressure, damaged steering rod, loose or worn front wheel bearings.

Front End Alignment

Front end alignment centers on the precise geometric relationship of a number of

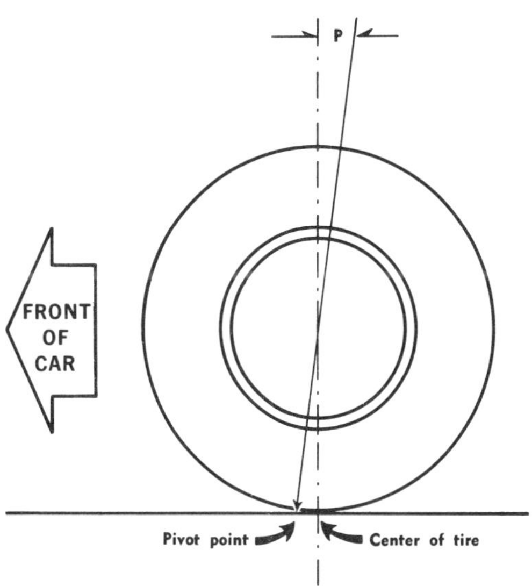

Front wheel caster. P = positive caster. The pivot point ahead of the center line of the tire holds the wheel stable.

parts—even when they are changing positions—that provides front wheel stability and control. These geometric angles include steering axis cant, caster, camber, included angle, toe-in, and toe-out (turning arc).

Before any adjustment is made, the condition of the complete front end system should be checked following the procedures given in the previous paragraphs and any defects corrected. Check the air pressure in all the tires. Check that the front tires are worn evenly. If not, replace or rotate them with the rear tires. Front wheel alignment must always be adjusted in this order: 1. Caster; 2. Camber; and 3. Toe-In.

Caster

Caster is the cant of the upper ball joint toward the rear of the car (positive). It gives the wheel another type of directional stability by moving the pivot point of the wheel forward of the tire's center. Positioning the pivot point ahead of center causes a drag on the bottom of the wheel (at the center) when it turns, thereby resisting the turn and tending to hold the wheel steady in whatever direction it has been going. The same principle of drag holds a weather vane pointer into the wind. The vane's bulky part seeks the point of minimum resistance behind the pivot.

Too slight a caster angle will cause the wheels to wander or weave at high speed and steer erratically when the brakes are applied. Too great a caster angle creates hard steering and shimmy at low speeds.

Camber

Camber is the angle that the centerline of the wheel makes with the vertical. The top of the wheel cants away from the car so that the center of the tire at the road lies at a point projected along the inclined axis of the upper and lower ball joints (steering axis cant). Placing the weight of the car directly over the pivot point allows easiest steering and takes some load off the outside wheel bearing.

Toe-out

Toe-out (turning arc) is the difference in angle of the two wheels in a turn. As the front end turns, the outside wheel describes a larger circle than does the inside wheel. The turning angle of each is, therefore, not the same and the difference of the two angles is toe-out. If all previously discussed front end angles and measurements are correct and yet toe-out is wrong, one or both of the steering arms are bent.

Toe-in

Usually measured in inches, this is the amount that both wheels are closer together at the front than at the rear. Toe-in is related to wheel camber and compres-

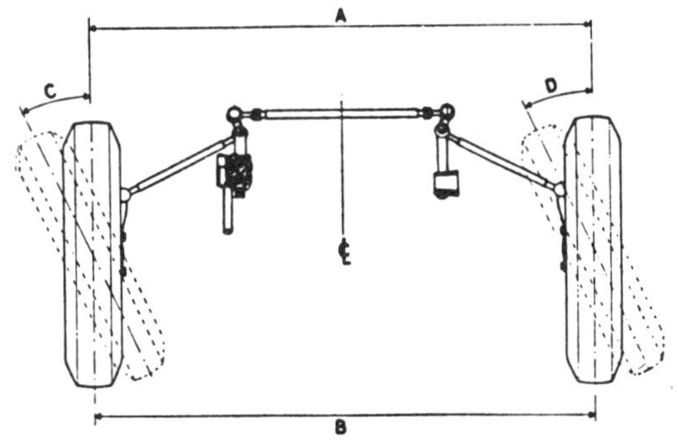

Toe-in = X—Y.

Adjusting caster and camber (144). A=Shims.

sion forces on the steering linkage with forward speed. The greater the camber, the greater is the toe-in, usually. Set toe-in only after checking caster and camber.

Steering Axis Cant

Steering axis cant, or kingpin inclination as termed years ago when kingpins were standard, is the angle (from the vertical) at which the steering knuckle is attached to the upper and lower ball joints. The canted steering knuckle controls wheel directional stability by forcing the wheel to lift the chassis in order to turn from a straight ahead direction. As the steering

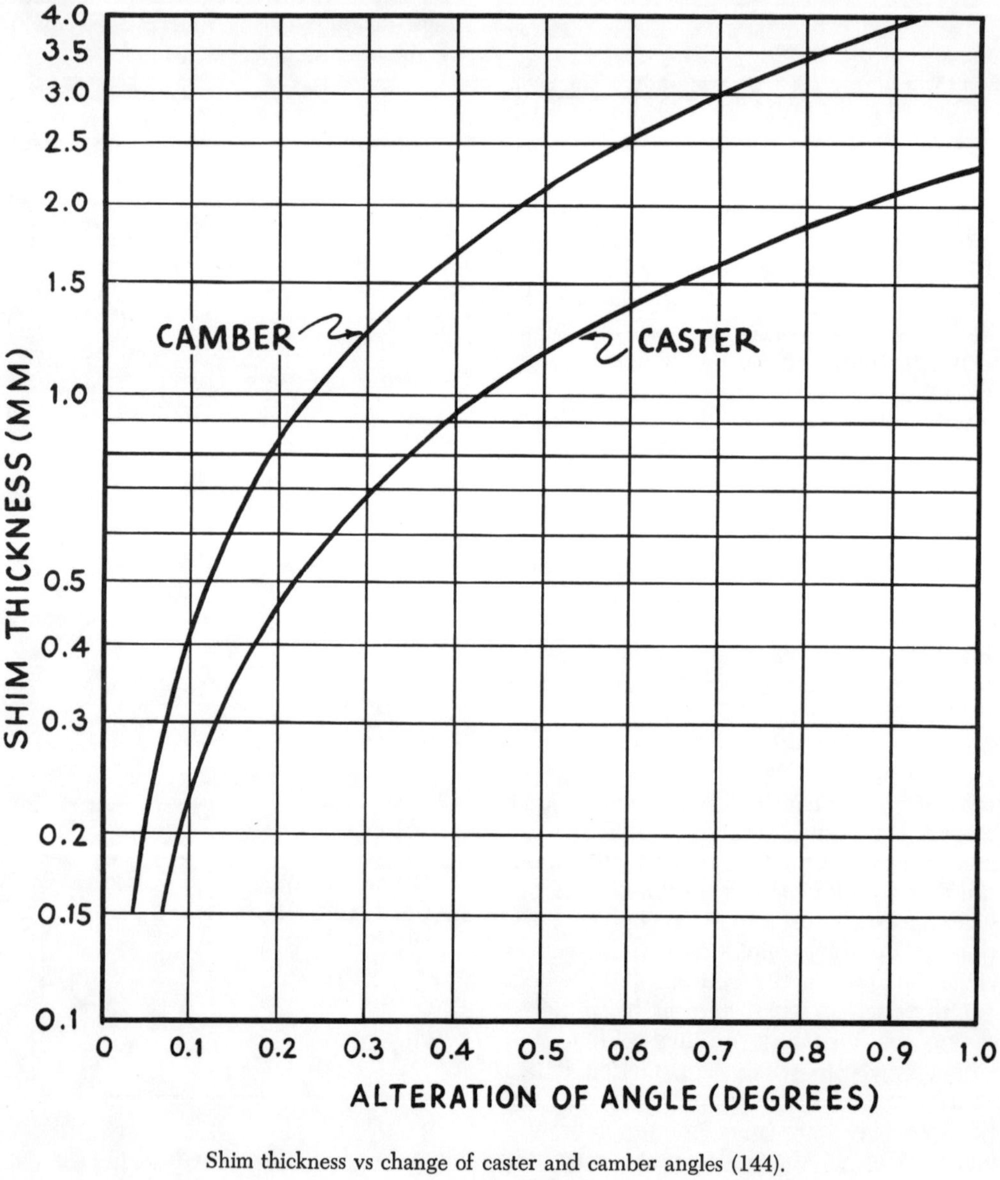

Shim thickness vs change of caster and camber angles (144).

arm releases its force over the wheel, the wheel returns to its straight ahead position under the force of the chassis weight. This inclination is not adjustable.

INCLUDED ANGLE

This is found by adding the steering axis cant to the positive wheel camber. This total must be equal on both front wheels regardless of what individual differences exist in axis cant and camber between the wheels. If the included angles of the two sides are different, a wheel spindle might be bent, possibly from striking a curb sharply.

Caster Adjustment (164, 145, 144, 1800, 122)

The caster should be 0° to + 1° and is adjusted by inserting or removing shims at the upper control arm shaft. Loosen the bolts several turns using SVO 2713, one end of which is used for the front bolt and the other for the rear bolt. Insert or remove shims as required.

Caster is increased toward the *positive* side either by inserting shims at the rear bolt, or by removing shims from the front bolt. For correct camber, the caster should be adjusted by transferring one-half the shim thickness (shown in diagram) from one bolt to the other, or simply by removing from one of the bolt positions the thickness indicated.

Tighten bolts before each measurement is made. When adjustment is complete, tighten bolts to a torque of 35–40 lb. ft.

Caster Adjustment (PV 444, 445, 544, P 122, 210)

The caster should be —¾° to +¼° and is adjusted by loosening the clamp bolt and turning the eccentric bushing with wrench SVO 1411 (early production) or wrench SVO 2201 (late production). One complete turn alters the caster angle by ½°. NOTE: if the wheel has the correct camber, one complete turn is necessary, otherwise the camber will be altered. Tighten clamp bolt each time before measuring caster.

Camber Adjustment (164, 145, 144, 1800, 122)

The camber should be 0° to +½° and is adjusted by use of shims in the upper control arm shaft. Loosen bolts a few turns with SVO 2713, one end of the wrench

1. Clamp bolt 2. Eccentric

Adjusting caster and camber (PV544).

being used for the front bolt and the other for the rear bolt. Then increase or decrease the number of shims equally at both the bolts. Camber positive angle is increased by removing shims and the negative angle increased by inserting shims. After each adjustment, tighten bolts before checking.

Camber Adjustment (PV 444, 445, 544, P 210)

After caster has been checked, camber can be adjusted to proper angle of —¼° to +½° by loosening the clamp bolt and turning the eccentric with wrench SVO 1411 or SVO 2201. An alteration of camber causes a slight but negligible change in caster.

Toe-In Adjustment

Toe-in should be 5⁄32″ and is adjusted by loosening the clamp bolts on the tie rod, and turning the rod in the required direction. Toe-in is increased by turning the rod in the direction of forward wheel rotation. Check caster and camber before adjusting toe-in.

King-Pin Inclination

King-pin inclination should be checked and should be 5° when the camber is 0°.

Wheel Balance

Front end alignment will not remain correct long if wheels are not balanced both dynamically and statically. See Chapter 1, under *Wheel and Tire Care.*

Chassis and Wheel Alignment Specifications

	Chassis		*Wheel Alignment*					
Model	*Wheelbase (In.)*	*Track (In.)*	*Caster (Deg.)*	*Camber (Deg.)*	*Toe-In (In.)*	*King Pin Inclin. (Deg.)*	*Wheel Pivot Ratio* Inner	*Wheel Pivot Ratio* Outer
PV444, PV445, PV544	102.5	51.0(F), 51.7(R)	-3/4 to +1/4	-1/4 to + 1/2	0 to .118	5	22 ±1	20
122	102.4	51.7	0 to +1	0 to +1/2	0 to .154	8		
142, 144, 145	102.4	53.1	0 to +1	0 to +1/2	0 to .16	7.5	21.5 to 23.5	20
164	106.3	53.2	0 to +1	0 to +1/2	0 to .16	7.5	21.5 to 23.5	20

Description

Volvo engines B14, B16, B18 and B20 are all four cylinder, water-cooled, overhead-valve, engines. The B30 is similar to the earlier series, differing mainly by having six cylinders. The B14 engine was superceded in 1958 by the B16 engine. The B18 engine was introduced in 1962 and the B20 in 1968. The B30, used in the 164, was introduced in 1969.

B18, B20 and B30 Engines

The B18 series of engines consists of Models B18A, B18B and B18 D. The B18A is provided with a Zenith 36VN down draft carburetor (some production models were provided with a horizontal Zenith-Stromberg 175CD2S), while the B18B and B18D models both have either twin Zenith-Stromberg 175-2SE or twin Horizontal SU-HS6 types. SAE bhp outputs are 75 @ 4500 rpm for the B18A; 100 @ 5500 for the B18B; and 90 @ 5000 for the B18D. B18B engines incorporate an oil cooler, positive crankcase ventilation and other design features not included on the B18A.

The B20 series consists of the B20A and B20B engines. The B20A, not imported to the U.S., has a single Zenith-Stromberg 175-CD-2SE carburetor, and the B20B, imported to the U.S., has either two Zenith-Stromberg 175-CD-2SE or two SU-HS6 carburetors. The B30 engine is equipped with two Zenith-Stromberg 175-CD-2SE carburetors.

The cylinder block is a single unit made of cast iron alloy. The machined cylinder bores are surrounded by cooling jackets. Oil openings are arranged so that the full-flow oil filter (with the oil cooler in B18B engines) is attached directly to the right side of the block.

The cylinder head is bolted to the block. All combustion chambers are machined with intake and exhaust valve ports and cooling water jackets. The overhead valves are made of special steel with chrome stems and are mounted in replaceable guides.

The crankshaft is drop forged steel with drilled oil ways and case hardened crankpins. There are five main bearings on the B18 and B20, seven on the B30, the rear bearing also functioning as a thrust bearing. The main bearings and bearing inserts of the B18, B20 and B30 engines are steel-backed, indium-plated lead bronze. Bearing inserts can be replaced without removing the engine.

A camshaft of special alloy cast iron and case hardened cams is driven from the crankshaft through a gear train which has a reduction ratio of 2:1. The camshaft is guided axially by a thrust washer at the front end. A shim behind the camshaft gear determines the clearance. Valve lifters are actuated directly by the camshaft. They are located in the block above the camshaft and transfer movement to the valves by means of push rods and rocker arms. There are no inspection covers for the valve lifters since they are accessible from above when the cylinder head is removed.

Connecting rods of drop forged steel are provided with precision-machined bushings which act as bearings for the wrist pins. Bearing inserts are replaceable. Pistons are made of light alloy and have two compression rings and one oil ring. The upper compression ring is chrome to reduce cylinder wear. The wrist pins are floating in both the piston and connecting rod. Axial movement of the wrist pin is limited by circlips in the wrist pin hole.

The engine employs a forced-feed lubricating system, pressure being provided by a pump driven by the camshaft and located in the oil pan under the crankshaft. The pump forces oil past a relief valve on the pump, through the oil filter and through oil passages to various lubricating points. All oil supplied to lubricating points, therefore, first passes through the oil filter.

The oil pump is a gear type. The pressure pipe from the pump to the cylinder block has no threads but is tightened in position when the pump bolts are secured. There are special rubber seals at each end of the pipe. The relief valve is mounted directly on the pump.

The oil filter is a full-flow type and on B18, B20 and B30 engines is mounted directly on the cylinder block. (On the B18B, an oil cooler is installed between the oil filter and the cylinder block. This is described in a later paragraph.) The filter element is made of special paper and should be replaced when it becomes dirty.

General Engine Specifications

Type	*Cu. In. Displacement (cc's)*	*Carburetion*	*SAE Horsepower @ rpm*	*Torque (ft. lbs.) @ rpm*	*Bore x Stroke (in.)*	*Compress. Ratio*	*Normal Oil Pressure (psi)*
B-14A	86 (1410)	Dual Sidedraft	70 @ 5,500	75.9 @ 3,000	2.953 x 3.150	7.8:1	43–57 @ 2,000
B-16A	96.4 (1580)	Single Downdraft	66 @ 4,500	86.5 @ 2,500	3.125 x 3.150	7.4:1	36–50 @ 2,000
B-16B	96.4 (1580)	Dual Sidedraft	85 @ 5,500	87 @ 3,500	3.125 x 3.150	8.2:1	36–50 @ 2,000
B-16D	96.4 (1580)		72 @ 5,500	86.1 @ 2,600	3.125 x 3.150	8.2:1	36–50 @ 2,000
B-18A	109 (1780)	Single Downdraft	75 @ 4,500	103 @ 2,800	3.313 x 3.150	8.5:1	50–85 @ 2,000
B-18B	109 (1780)	Dual Sidedraft	100 @ 5,500	108 @ 4,000	3.313 x 3.150	9.5:1	50–85 @ 2,000
B-18D	109 (1780)	Dual Sidedraft	90 @ 5,000	105 @ 3,500	3.313 x 3.150	8.5:1	50–85 @ 2,000
B-20A	122 (1990)	Single Sidedraft	90 @ 4,800	119 @ 3,000	3.50 x 3.150	8.7:1	36–85 @ 2,000
B-20B	122 (1990)	Dual Sidedraft	118 @ 5,800	123 @ 3,500	3.50 x 3.150	9.5:1	36–85 @ 2,000
B-30A	183 (2980)	Dual Sidedraft	145 @ 5,500	163 @ 3,000	3.50 x 3.150	9.2:1	36–85 @ 2,000

The oil filter contains a valve which allows oil to bypass the element if resistance to flow becomes excessive.

The oil cooler on B18B engines is installed between the oil filter and cylinder block and consists of an oil duct surrounded by a water cooling jacket. Baffles in the paths of the oil and cooling water conduct heat away from the oil.

The B18, B20 and B30 engines are equipped with positive crankcase ventilation, which prevents crankcase gases from being released into the atmosphere. Instead the gases are sucked into the combustion chambers of the engine through the intake manifold. Between the crankcase and intake manifold, there is a connection which consists of two rubber hoses and an oil trap attached to the valve inspection cover. One of the hoses contains a valve and is connected between the oil trap and the intake manifold. The valve controls the flow of gases sucked into the intake manifold from the crankcase and also acts as a check valve to prevent carburetor backfire from reaching the crankcase. The other hose is connected between the oil filler cap on the rocker arm casing and the carburetor air filter and supplies fresh filtered air to the crankcase. The oil filler cap has a built in flame trap which, like the control valve, prevents backfire from reaching the rocker arm casing. At full engine load, when the partial vacuum in the crankcase is less than that in the air filter, air flow from the filter to the rocker arm casing reverses and crankcase gases then go through both hoses to the intake manifold. Thus, the PCV can handle relatively large volumes of crankcase gas.

The distributor which is driven by a bevel gear from the crankshaft has both a centrifugal and vacuum regulator. The direction of rotation is counterclockwise and the firing order is 1-3-4-2 for the B18 and B20, 1-5-3-6-2-4 for the B30.

B14 and B16 Engines

This series of engines consists of Models B14A, B16A, B16B and B16D. The B14A is equipped with twin SU-H2 horizontal carburetors, while the B16A and B16D each have a single Zenith 34VN down draft carburetor. The B16B is equipped with twin SU-H4 horizontal carburetors which are somewhat larger than those on the B14A. SAE bhp outputs are 70 @ 5500 rpm for the B14A; 66 @ 4500 for the B16A; 85 @ 5500 for the B15B; and 72 @ 5500 for the B16D.

The cylinder block is a single unit made of cast iron alloy. The machined cylinder bores are surrounded by cooling jackets. Oil openings are arranged in the B16A, B16B and B16D blocks so that the oil filter is attached directly to the side of the engine. The oil filter on B14A engines is connected to the engine by external lines. The crankshaft is drop forged steel with case hardened crankpins. There are three main bearings, the rear bearing also functioning as a thrust bearing. Undersize inserts are available to provide the correct clearance for reground journals, and bearing inserts can be replaced without removing the engine. The main bearings and connecting rod bearings (except on the B16A) are steel-backed, indium-plated lead bronze. On the B16A engine, connecting rod bearings are special lead-bronze alloy, while the main bearings are babbit lined. A camshaft of special steel with hardened cams is guided axially by a thrust washer at the front end.

Pistons are made of light alloy and have two compression rings and one oil ring. The upper compression ring is chrome to reduce cylinder wear. Pistons contain a stamping on the top to indicate direction of installation. Connecting rods of drop forged steel are provided with precision-machined bearings and bushings. Bearing inserts are replaceable. The wrist pins are floating in both the piston and connecting rod. Axial movement of the wrist pin is limited by circlips in the wrist pin hole.

The engine employs a forced feed lubricating system, pressure being supplied by a pump driven by the camshaft. The pump forces oil first through the filter and then through oil passages to the various points. On the B16 engines, the oil filter is attached directly to the side of the block. The B14A oil filter is connected to the oil system by external lines. The filter element is made of special paper and should be replaced when it becomes dirty. A valve in the oil filter allows oil to bypass the element if resistance to flow becomes excessive. The distributor which is driven by a bevel gear from the crankshaft has both a centrifugal and vacuum regulator. Ignition timing on the B14A engine can be retarded or advanced by a screw adjustment on the distributor. The direction of rotation is counterclockwise and the firing order is 1-3-4-2. Top dead center is indicated by markings on the flywheel and pulley, and a raised spot on the timing gear casing.

Engine Components and Assemblies

The following paragraphs give procedures for removal of engine components and assemblies for repair or replacement without removing the engine from the vehicle.

Water Pump Replacement

1. Drain the cooling system by opening one drain cock on the radiator and one on the rear right side of the engine.
2. Loosen the fan belt by loosening the generator mounting bolts, and disconnect the water pipes.
3. Remove the pump, noting the position of the sealing rings on top of the pump so that they can be replaced in the same position.
4. Before installing new pump, make sure the sealing rings are in good condition and are pushed into the pipe thoroughly. Press the pump upward against the cylinder head extension while bolting into position so that there is a good seal.
5. Fill the cooling system and test run the engine for leakage.

Thermostat Replacement

Remove the bolts from the flange in the upper water line which houses the thermostat, and turn the pipe up and out of the way. Replace the thermostat using a new gasket. Position the water pipe, install the bolts and fill cooling system. Check for leaks.

Oil Filter Replacement

The oil filter is screwed onto a nipple in the block on B18A, B20 and B30 engines. On B18B engines, it screws onto a nipple in the air cooler.

B18, B20 and B30 Engines

Remove the old filter by turning with the hands or with a chain wrench. Discard old filter. Coat the rubber gasket of the new filter with oil and make sure both contacting surfaces are clean. Screw on the filter by hand until it just comes to the end of its travel. Then screw in the filter a further half-turn by hand. *Do not use the chain wrench for tightening the filter.* Start engine and check for oil leaks.

B16 Engines

Loosen the center bolt on the oil filter housing, being prepared to collect the oil that runs out. Remove the oil filter. Discard the old element and clean the filter housing. Insert the new element (observing the "up" marking) and gasket in the housing, and bolt filter unit to side of engine, guiding it with the hand so that it fits into the groove correctly. Tighten bolt to torque of 15 lb. ft. (2 kgm). Add 1½ pints of oil to the crankcase for the new filter element. Start the engine and check for oil leaks.

B14 Engines

Drain filter by removing oil plug from the side of the filter support. Loosen center bolt on oil filter housing and remove filter. Discard old filter element and clean filter housing. Install new filter element. Install drain plug and attached oil filter assembly to support. Add 1½ pints of oil to crankcase for new filter element. Run engine and check for oil leaks.

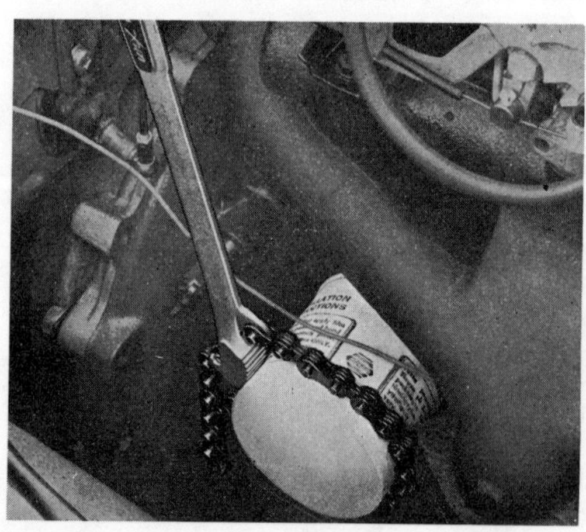

Removing oil filter.

fall. Next turn the rear cover so that it locks the reverse shaft and install the cover bolts. For overdrive types, make sure that the cam for the overdrive oil pump is turned upwards. Install the overdrive. Use new lock washers for the intermediate flange.

Install selector rails and forks. Move selector fork to rear position and install new pin. Install cover over selector rails. (NOTE: if the end caps at front of housing have been removed, they should be installed as before, with center and cap projecting about 5/32″ outside the housing.) Place interlock balls and springs in position. Install cover. Check that all gears engage and disengage freely. Install transmission in reverse order to removal. Fill with transmission lubricant.

Transmission Disassembly—M400

Remove the overdrive unit if so equipped. Mount the transmission in stand and jig SVO 2520 and SVO 2825 or equivalent. Remove the cover, springs and interlock balls for the selector rails. Remove the flange using wrench SVO 2837 and puller SVO 2261. Remove the release bearing. Remove the cover for the input shaft and the clutch housing. Turn the gearbox upside down and pull out the front bearing for the intermediate shaft with tool SVO 2826. Remove the rear cover and pull out the rear bearing of the intermediate shaft with tool SVO 2827.

Turn the gearbox upright, but be careful that the teeth of the intermediate shaft are not damaged as it drops to the bottom of the gearbox. Unscrew the bolts for the selector forks. Push the selector rails backward and drive out the tensioning pin in the flange of the selector rails and the selector rails. Hold the forks while removing the rails so they do not jam as the rails are removed and then remove the forks.

Remove the speedometer gear. Pull out the rear bearing of the mainshaft with tool SVO 2828. For the M410, remove the bolt in the puller and replace it with SVO 2832 and pull out the bearing.

Pull out the input shaft and remove the synchronizing ring. Remove the thrust washer from the mainshaft rear end. Fit lifting tool SVO 2829 or a rope or sling on the mainshaft. Push the engaging sleeve for 1st and 2nd gear rearward and lift out the mainshaft. Pull out the reverse shaft with puller SVO 2830. Remove the oil seals.

1. Roller
2. Pump lunger
3. Spring
4. Lever
5. Pump cylinder
6. Ball
7. Valve seating
8. Spring
9. O ring
10. Valve seating, relief valve
11. Spring
12. Valve plunger
13. Lever
14. Piston
15. Armature for solenoid
16. Valve rod (cutaway view)
17. Plunger seal
18. Solenoid
19. Thrust bearing retainer
20. Housing, rear part
21. Bushing
22. Speedometer gear, small
23. Ball bearing
24. Thrust washer
25. Output shaft
26. Coupling flange
27. Sealing ring
28. Ball bearing
29. Spacing sleeve
30. Speedometer gear, large
31. Needle bearing
32. Thrust washer
33. Freewheel rollers
34. Freewheel hub
35. Oil deflector plate
36. Lock ring
37. Oil catcher
38. Planet gear
39. Needle bearing
40. Clutch facing
41. Brake drum
42. Locking pin
43. Clutch disc
44. Shaft
45. Planet gear carrier
46. Sunwheel
47. Ball bearing
48. Housing, front part
49. Plug over control valve
50. Pressure plate
51. Breather nipple
52. Tappet (cutaway)
53. Ball (cutaway)
54. Spring
55. Bushing
56. Pressure plate
57. Cam
58. Extension piece
59. Input shaft (mainshaft)
60. Rear cover, gearbox

Mainshaft Disassembly

Remove the 1st speed gear, needle bearing and synchronizer cone. Remove the engaging sleeves and flanges for the synchronizers. Remove the snap-rings from the synchronizer hub. With tool SVO 2853 or equivalent, press off the 2nd speed gear and the 1st and 2nd speed synchronizer hub. Turn the shaft over and press off the 3rd speed gear and the 3rd and 4th speed synchronizer hub. Assemble the mainshaft in the reverse order of the above procedure.

Transmission Assembly

Insert front and rear oil seals into the front and rear covers. Press the ball bearing onto the input shaft with tool SVO 2851 and SVO 2852 or equivalent. Fit a snap-ring into the groove. Place the lever for the reverse shaft onto the bearing pin. Fit the reverse gear and shaft. The reverse shaft should be flush within 0.08 in. (0.2 mm.) of the rear of the housing.

Place the intermediate shaft in the bottom of the gearbox housing. Fit the mainshaft in the housing and install a thrust washer. Press the ball bearing onto the mainshaft using press SVO 2831 or equivalent.

Fit the needle bearing in the input shaft. Install the loose synchronizer cone in the 3rd and 4th speed synchronizer hub. Align the flanges in the grooves. Push the input shaft into the housing and onto the pin of the mainshaft.

Turn the gearbox upside down and insert the intermediate shaft bearing with tool SVO 2831 or equivalent. Fit the clutch housing with a new gasket. Turn the gearbox right side up and install the selector forks, flanges and rails. Make sure the flange for the reverse gear fits correctly in the gear lever. Fit the bolts and new tensioning pins.

With the rear end of the gearbox facing up, push the intermediate shaft forward so the front bearing lies against the clutch housing. Fit shims under the intermediate shaft bearing to give a clearance of from 0.002 in. (0.05 mm.) below to even with the rear of the case. Fit the speedometer gear and rear cover with new gasket. Clearance between the intermediate shaft and the rear cover is 0.008 to 0.010 in. (0.2 to 0.25 mm.). Press on the flange with tool SVO 1845, and install the washer and nut to 80 to 110 ft. lbs. (11 to 14 kgm.) of torque. Place the interlocking balls and springs in position. Replace the gearbox and front cover with new gaskets.

Overdrive

Overdrive for the M31 and M40 transmissions is of the planetary gear type and is mounted on the rear end of the transmission. In driving forward, power from the transmission mainshaft is transmitted through the freewheel rollers to the overdrive output shaft. When reversing or using the engine as a brake, power is transmitted through the clutch disc which is held by spring pressure against the tapered portion of the output shaft. In overdrive, the clutch disc is pressed against the brake drum, in which position the sun wheel is locked. When driving, the planet gears rotate around the sun wheel. As a result, the output shaft rotates at higher speed than the mainshaft.

Overdrive is actuated by a switch under the steering wheel or on the instrument panel. This switch energizes a solenoid on the overdrive unit via a switch on the transmission, which is cut in when the 4th speed is engaged. The solenoid has two windings, a heavy control winding and a lower current, "hold" winding. The control winding causes the solenoid to open a valve, whereupon the control winding is cut off and the valve is held open by the hold winding. The valve controls the flow of oil pressure from a cam-operated pump to hydraulic cylinders which operate the overdrive clutch disc.

OVERDRIVE REMOVAL

Remove transmission as described previously. Drain oil from overdrive and disconnect cable to solenoid. Remove bolts which hold overdrive to intermediate flange and remove overdrive unit. Replace unit in reverse order and fill with lubricant. Since specialized testing equipment and tools are required for servicing the overdrive unit, it is best to have a qualified Volvo service department do any repair work necessary.

Chapter 8
Drive Shaft and Rear Axle

Drive Shaft

The drive shaft for the Volvo PV444 up to chassis number 2505 is in one piece. Starting with chassis number 2506 on the PV 444, and for the PV 445, 544, P 210, 144 and 164, the drive shaft is made in two pieces and has three Hardy-Spicer universal joints equipped with needle bearings.

Drive Shaft Removal

The front and rear sections of the drive shaft can be removed in one piece by disconnecting the universal joints at the transmission and at the rear axle, and then pulling the two sections out backwards at the same time. However, to remove either the rear or front section, or both, the following procedure is used.

Disconnect front universal joint of rear section of drive shaft by removing the four bolts in the flange behind the support bearing. Be careful not to drop end of shaft, for it can be damaged easily. Disconnect rear universal joint at pinion driving flange in the same manner, and remove rear section of drive shaft.

After the rear section has been removed, punch mating marks on flange and shaft and disconnect the front universal of the front section by removing the bolts from the flange of the transmission shaft. The drive shaft with universal joint and bearing housing can then be removed by pulling out backwards.

Drive Shaft Disassembly

If front and rear sections of shaft are assembled, bend back tabs of lock washer and remove nut for support bearing. Remove rear section of shaft. Pull off the support bearing.

Universal Joint Disassembly

Remove lock rings which hold needle bearings in the yokes. Tighten shaft in vise being careful not to deform it. With a hammer and thick steel punch, drive the spider as far as it will go in the opposite direction. The needle bearing will then come about half way out. Then drive the spider as far as it will go in the other direction. Drive out one of the needle bearings with a thinner punch. Remove the spider and then drive out the other needle bearing.

Inspect the shaft. It must be straight, or it can cause vibration. An indicator gauge should be used for checking while the

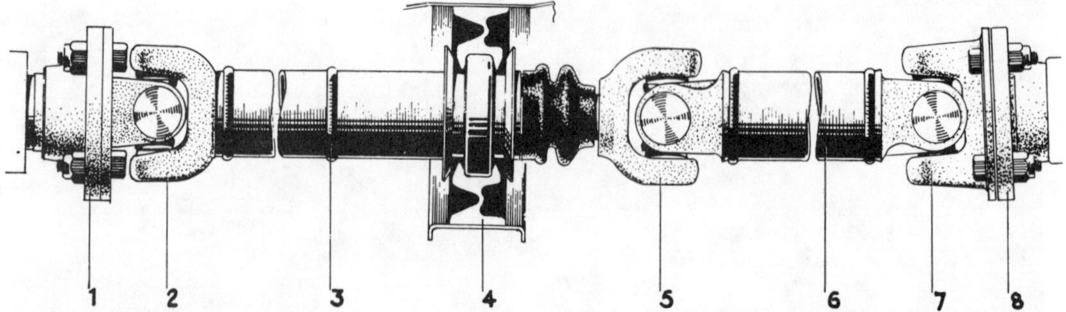

1. Transmission flange
2. Front universal
3. Front section of drive shaft
4. Support bearing
5. Intermediate universal
6. Rear section of drive shaft
7. Rear universal
8. Rear axle flange

Drive shaft components.

1. Driving flange
2. Bearing housing
3. Splash guard
4. Center punch
5. Bolt

Marking drive shaft and flange.

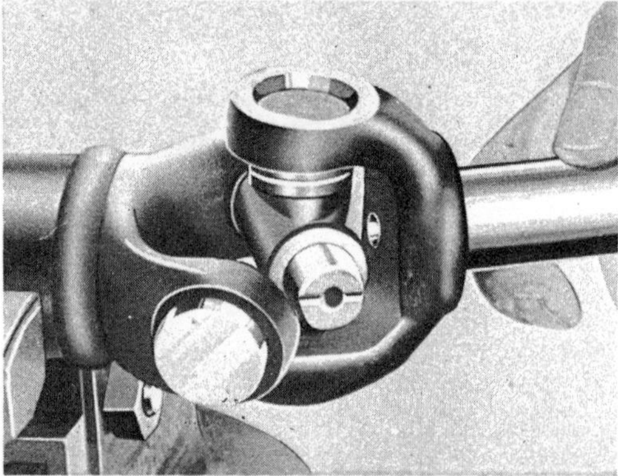

Removing needle bearings.

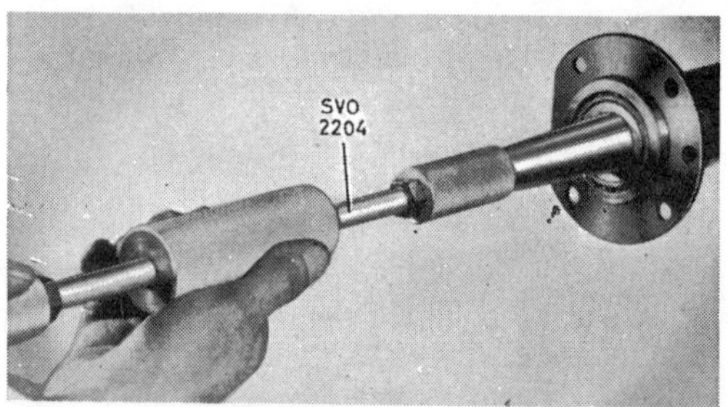

Removing rear axle.

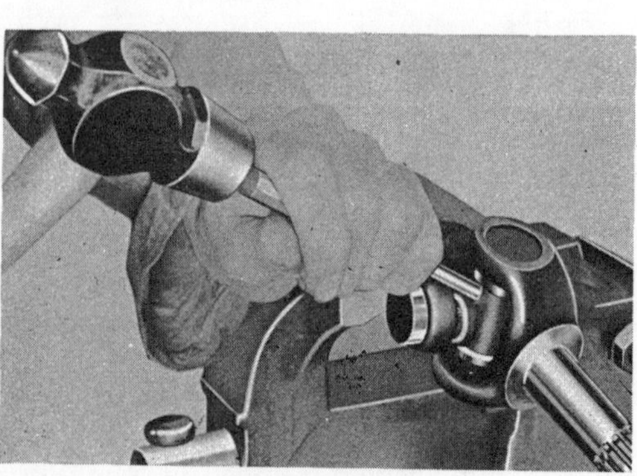

Removing spider.

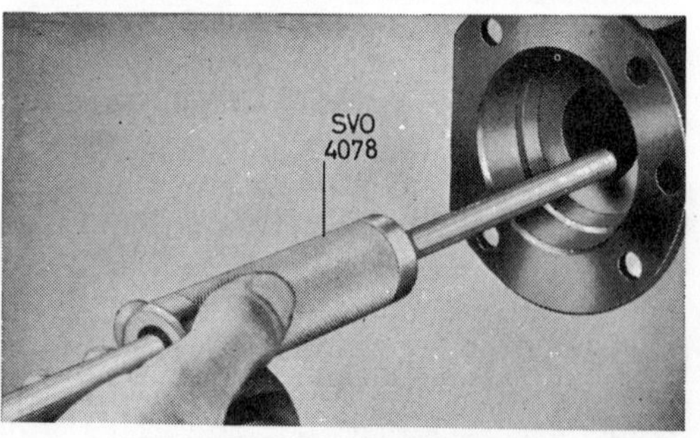

Removing rear axle oil seal.

shaft is rotated. If it is out by more than .010″ the shaft must be replaced. No attempt should be made to straighten a bent shaft.

Examine support bearing by pressing races toward each other with the hand and turning them in opposite directions. If the bearing binds or does not run easily, replace it. Check needle bearings and spiders for wear or damage.

Drive Shaft Assembly

Check that needle bearings are half-filled with grease. Insert spider in flange yoke, pushing the spider over in one direction far enough so that needle bearing can be installed onto trunnion. Then with a drift, press in needle bearing so that lock ring can be inserted. Install other needle bearings and spiders in the same way. Install drive shaft on vehicle in reverse order to removal.

Rear Axle

Hypoid gears are employed in PV 544, P 1800, P 120, 144S, 164 and in PV 444, starting with Chassis 8378. The principle of rear axle suspension is utilized. Each axle is supported at its outer end by a tapered bearing. Differential bearing lateral adjustment is made by inserting or removing shims between the housing and the differential side bearings. Axle end play is determined by shims between the brake backing plate and the end of the axle housing.

Rear axle shafts, bearings, oil seals and the pinion oil seal at the front of the housing can be replaced without removing the axle and rear housings from the vehicle.

Axle, Oil Seal and Wheel Bearing Replacement

Remove wheel and pull off wheel hub. Avoid getting oil or grease on brake linings. Place a wooden block under the brake pedal and disconnect brake line from backing plate.

Pull axle, using puller SVO 2204. Remove oil seal with puller SVO 4078. Drive in new oil seal, making sure it is correctly positioned.

Press off bearing, using SVO 1806 under the bearing. Install new bearing with SVO 1805 and pack with grease. Remove any oil or grease from the brake

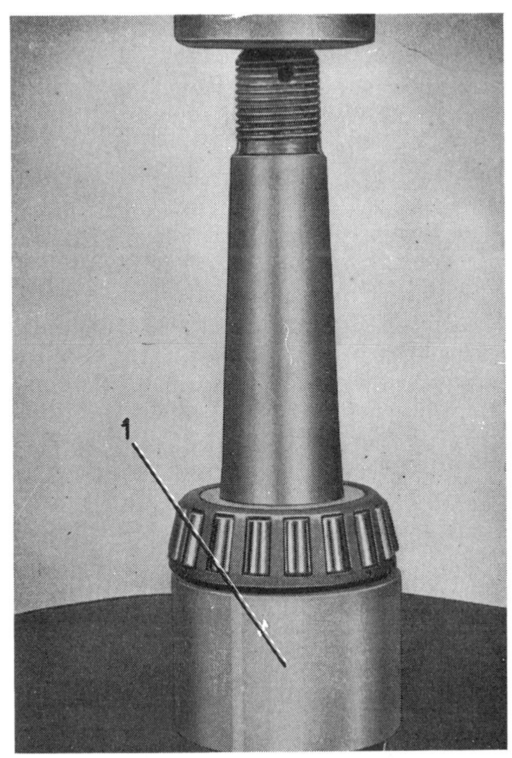

Removing rear axle bearing. 1 = Tool SVO 1806.

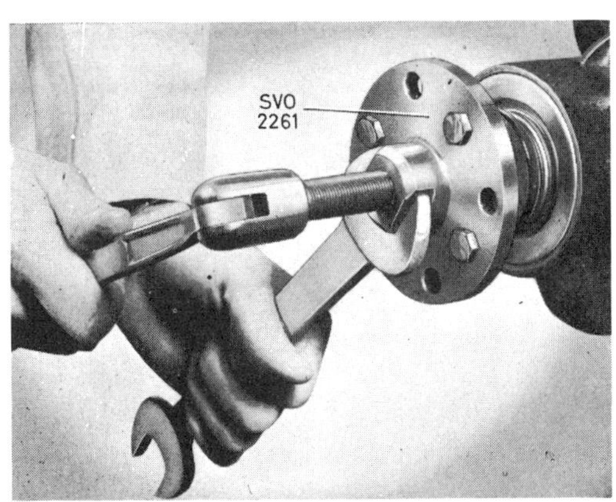

Removing pinion flange.

backing plate. Install axle and brake backing plate with a new felt washer. Replace draw key if it has been removed, and install hub and wheel. Bleed brake lines and adjust brakes. Check oil level in rear, and add oil if necessary.

Pinion Oil Seal Replacement

Disconnect rear section of drive shaft from pinion flange. Remove flange nut using SVO 2409 as a counterhold. Pull flange with SVO 2261. Remove old oil seal with SVO 4030 and install new oil seal with new paper gasket using tool SVO 2403. Press on flange with SVO 1845 and install washer and nut. Tighten to a torque of 200-220 lb.-ft. Reconnect drive shaft.

Axle and Rear Housing Removal

Place blocks in front of the front wheels. Drain rear. Loosen rear wheel nuts. Place special rear axle fixture SVO 2714 on a heavy-duty jack and lift under rear housing. Place supports under body slightly forward of rear wheels. Remove rear flange on rear. Disconnect brake line from master cylinder (place wooden block under brake pedal). Disconnect hand-brake cables and brackets on brake backing plate. Loosen track bar, upper shock absorber bolts and shock absorber straps from axle. Loosen nuts for support arms. Lower the rear axle and remove springs. Loosen bolts for torque rods and remove rear axle. Clean rear axle externally and allow oil to drain off.

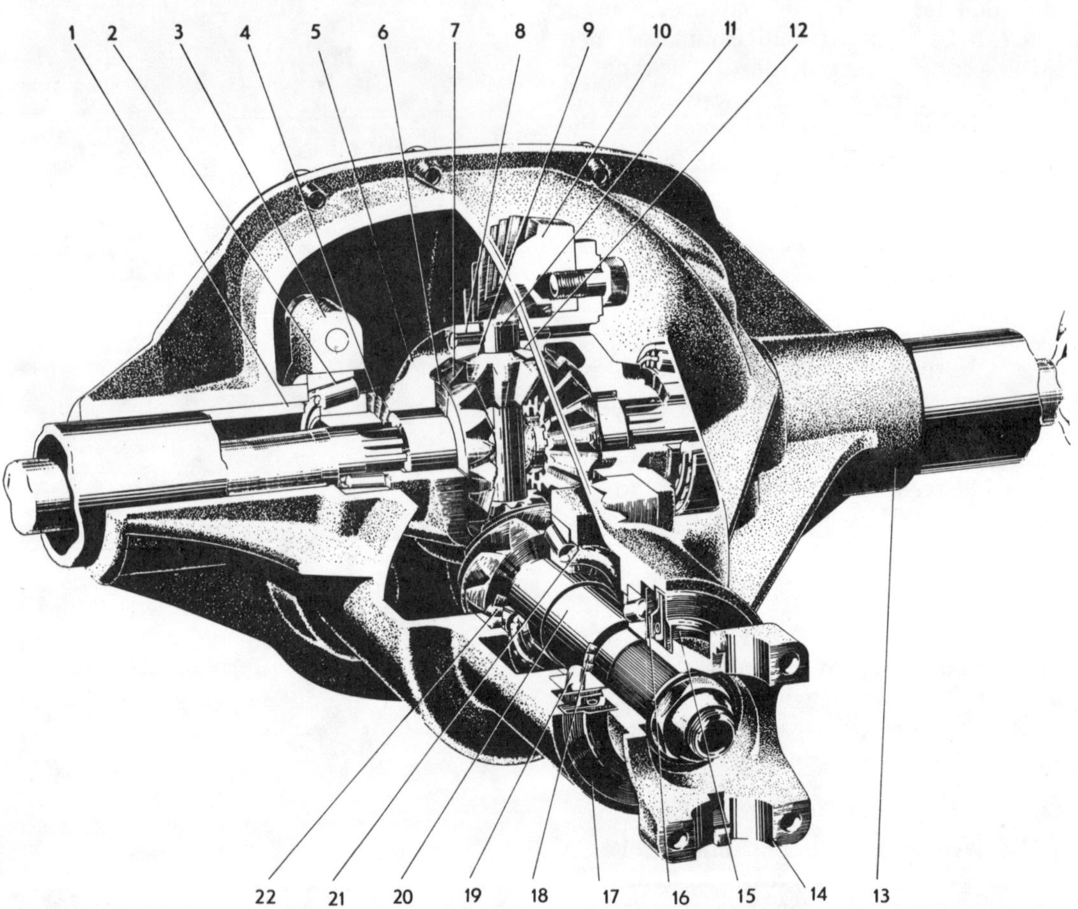

1. Tubular shaft
2. Differential shaft
3. Bearing cap
4. Shims
5. Differential carrier
6. Thrust washer
7. Differential gear
8. Lock pin
9. Differential pinion
10. Ring gear
11. Shaft
12. Thrust washer
13. Axle housing
14. Pinion flange
15. Dust cover plate
16. Oil slinger
17. Pinion oil seal
18. Shims
19. Front pinion bearing
20. Pinion
21. Rear pinion bearing
22. Shims

Rear axle and differential (144).

Description, Removal and Repair

The front end of the Volvo employs independent front wheel suspension with coil springs. Support is provided by upper and lower control arms pivoted on a front axle member bolted to the frame or body. The upper and lower arms support the shock absorber, and the lower arm and front axle members support the coil spring. The steering knuckle is carried in king pins between the arms. Stabilizer bars are attached to the lower control arm and frame. Coil springs are used also in the rear.

Front Wheel Suspension

Front Wheel Alignment

(See Chapter Two—"Front End Troubleshooting")

Wheel Bearing Replacement

(Tools for PV 444, 445, 544, and P210 are shown in parenthesis). Loosen wheel nuts slightly before jacking, then jack up front end and place blocks under the lower control arms. Remove wheel. For 164 and 144 models, remove brake caliper by disconnecting brake lines and removing mounting bolts. Remove grease cap, cotter pin and wheel nut. Pull hub with SVO 2726 (SVO 1791, 1446). Pull inner bearing from wheel axle with SVO 2722 (SVO 1794, 4016) if the bearing remains in place. Remove inner bearing race with drift SVO 2724 (SVO 1799, 4003) and outer clearing race with drift SVO 2725 (SVO 1800, 4002) together with handle SVO 1801. Clean hub, grease cap, brake disc and drum.

Press in new bearings with drift SVO 2723 (SVO 1798, 4001) for the inner race and SVO 2724 (SVO 1797, 4000) for the outer race together with handle SVO 1801. Pack bearings full of grease, applying grease to outer sides of bearings and on outer races pressed into hub. Fill recess in hub with grease all around up to the smallest diameter of the outer race on the outer bearing. Insert inner bearing into position in hub and press in seal with SVO 2723 (SVO 1798, 4001) and handle SVO 1801. Place hub on axle. Install outer bearing, washer and wheel nut.

Adjust wheel bearings by first tighten-

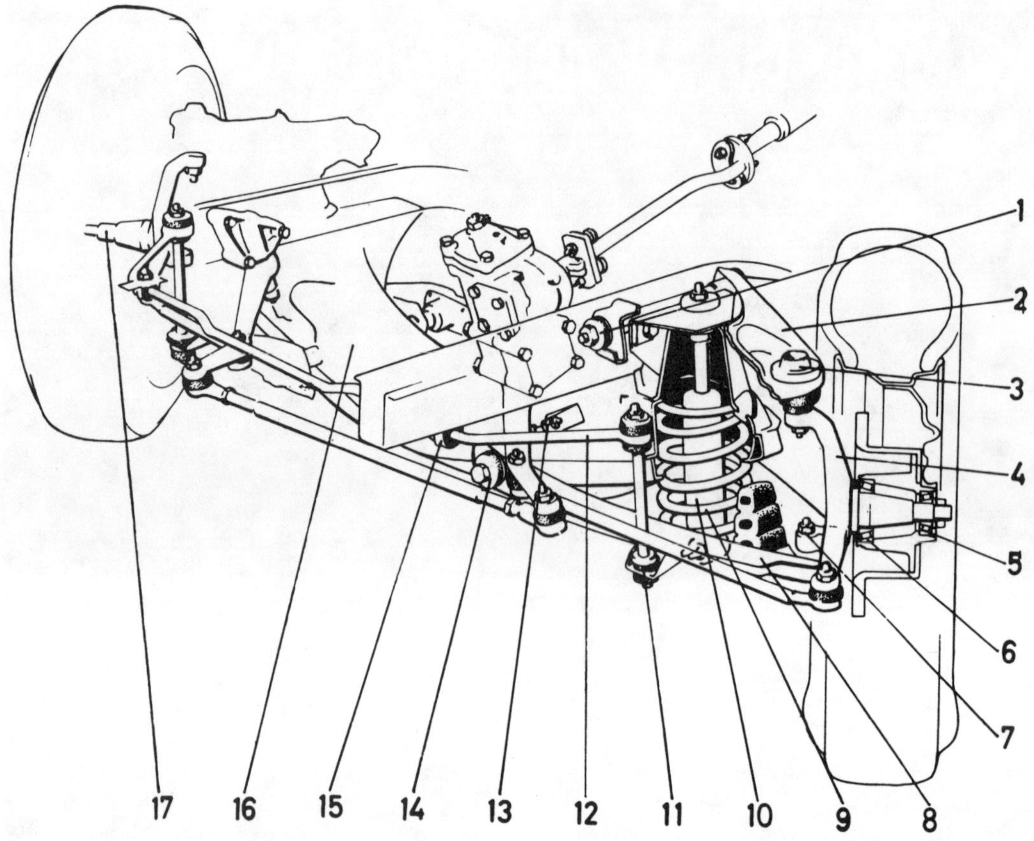

1. Upper control arm bushing
2. Upper control arm
3. Upper control arm ball joint
4. Steering knuckle
5. Outer wheel bearing
6. Inner wheel bearing
7. Lower control arm ball joint
8. Lower control arm
9. Coil spring
10. Shock absorber
11. Stabilizer attachment
12. Stabilizer
13. Stop screw max. wheel lock
14. Lower control arm bushing
15. Frame attachment for stabilizer
16. Front axle member
17. Front wheel axle

Front suspension, 144.

ing wheel nut to a torque of 50 lbs. ft. Then loosen nut one-third turn and install cotter pin. Check that wheel rotates easily without play. Half fill the grease cap and install. Install brake caliper and connect brake lines. Install wheel and tighten wheel nuts.

King Pin Replacement

Loosen wheel nuts slightly, and then jack up front end and place blocks under the lower control arms. Remove wheel and wheel hub as described previously under "Wheel Bearing Replacement," removing inner bearing race if necessary. Remove four bolts that hold brake backing plate in place and splash guard to steering knuckle. Lift off brake backing plate and tie up to avoid straining brake line.

Remove cotter pin and nut from steering arm ball joint. Place SVO 2294 on the ball joint, making sure the thread of the ball joint enters the countersink in the tool. Turn tensioning screw until ball joint releases. Loosen nut and unscrew upper control arm bolt. Remove clamping bolt and eccentric bushing. Disconnect shock absorber at bottom. Lift off steering knuckle support. Screw out lower bushing.

Drive out king pin stop key, and remove sealing washer with a pointed punch. Drive king pin downwards and

1. Steering knuckle support
2. Upper control arm
3. Steering gear housing
4. Stabilizer
5. Pitman arm
6. Front axle member
7. Steering rod and tie rod
8. Lower control arm
9. Coil spring
10. Shock absorber
11. Steering knuckle
12. Steering arm

Front suspension, 544.

Removing inner wheel bearing.

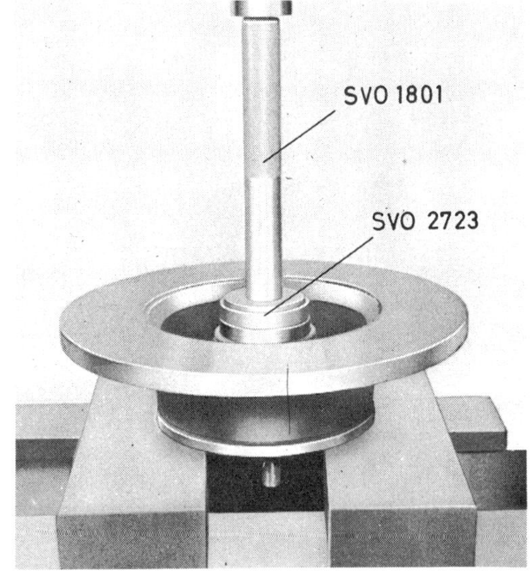

Installing inner wheel bearing seal.

out with SVO 2224. Remove grease fittings and drive out king pin bushings with SVO 1442.

Press in new bushings with SVO 1442. Make sure lubricating holes line up with grease fitting holes, and that the short lubricating groove faces the sealing washer. Ream bushings with SVO 1171. Install grease fittings. Coat bushings with chassis grease.

Position the axle steering knuckle, thrust bearing and adjusting shims, and place the centering mandrel SVO 4005 in the upper bushing. Change shims until the takeup corresponds to a friction torque of 4.34–56.4 lb. in. when turning the axle. This would be a reading of 0.66–9.46 lbs. on a spring scale attached to the cotter pin hole in the axle and pulled at right angles to the axle. Drive in king pin, making sure of correct position. Insert stop key. Check to see that steering knuckle turns easily. Install sealing washers with convex side out, then knock them flat with a hammer and drift pin.

Install steering knuckle support with bushings, guard plate and bolts. Connect steering rod to steering arm. Turn ball joint so that cotter pin hole lines longitudinally with rod. Tighten castle nut to a torque of 23-27 lb. ft. Install brake backing plate and splash plate on steering knuckle. Install hub and wheel, reversing previous steps for removal. Adjust wheel bearings and check front wheel alignment.

Upper Arm, Ball Joint Replacement (164, 144)

Jack up front end of vehicle and remove wheel. Loosen nut for upper control arm ball joint. With a hammer, tap the axle around the ball joint pin until it is loosened from the axle. Remove nut completely and suspend upper end of axle to avoid straining brake lines. Loosen control arm nuts one-half turn, lift arm slightly and press out ball joint with SVO 2699 and sleeve SVO 2701.

Before installing new ball joint, see that rubber cover is filled with grease. Bend the pin end over the slot, and be sure that the grease forces its way out. Press ball joint into control arm with SVO 2699, sleeve SVO 2701 and drift 2704, making sure that slot in ball joint lines up longitudinally with shaft of control arm either externally or internally, for the pin has maximum movement in the direction of this line. Should the ball joint be incorrectly positioned, turn the tool half a turn and then press the ball joint into the right position. Turn down the control arm and tighten the nuts on the control arm shaft. Tighten ball joint against axle. If the pin rotates, hold it with a C-clamp. Install front wheel.

Lower Arm, Ball Joint Replacement (164, 144)

Jack up front end of vehicle and remove wheel. Disconnect steering rod from steering arm with SVO 2294, and disconnect brake lines from stabilizer bolt. Slightly loosen nuts on upper and lower ball joints. With a hammer, tap ball joints loose from axle. Raise lower control arm with a jack. Remove nuts. Remove steering knuckle with hub and front wheel brake unit, and place the assembly on an elevated support near enough to avoid

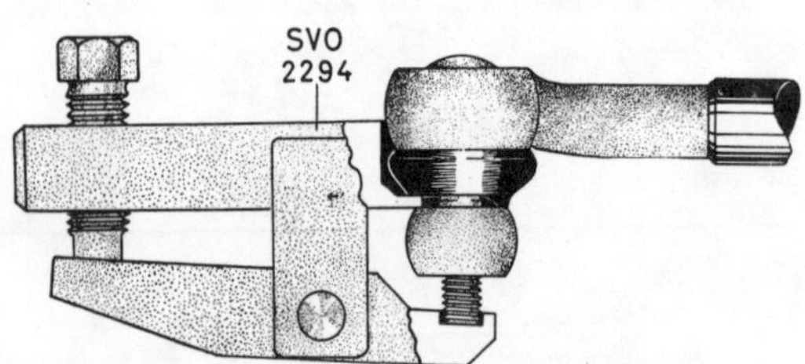

Removing steering rod ball joint.

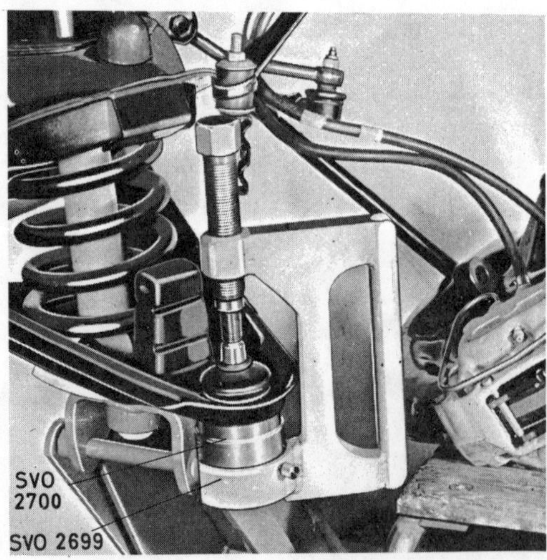

Removing ball joint, upper control arm.

strain on brake lines. Using tools SVO 2699 and SVO 2700, press ball joint out of lower arm. Before installing new joint, check to see that rubber cover is filled with grease by breaking the pin to the side, forcing the grease out. Fill with grease if necessary. Press new ball joint into position in control arm. Install steering knuckle and tighten upper and lower ball joints. Install steering rod, connect brake lines to stabilizer bolt and install front wheel.

Front Spring and Shock Absorber Replacement (164, 144)

Jack front end of vehicle and place on blocks. Remove shock absorber by removing upper nut, washer and rubber bushing. Remove two screws at bottom on underside of lower control arm and take out shock absorber.

Disconnect steering rod from steering arm and loosen clamp for brake lines. Remove stabilizer attachment. Place a jack under the lower control arm. Loosen nuts on ball joints, and tap with hammer until ball joints loosen from wheel axle. Remove nuts. Remove steering knuckle with front wheel brake. Lower jack and remove spring. Install new spring in reverse order of above.

Front Spring Replacement (PV 444, 544)

Jack front end of vehicle and place on blocks. Disconnect stabilizer. Place jack under lower control arm, and loosen four nuts on front axle support member bracket. Lower jack slowly and remove spring. Install new spring in reverse order of above, making sure that new ring is in correct position, with the straight end resting in the recess in the lower spring attachment. Check front wheel alignment and if necessary readjust (See Chapter Two).

Rear Suspension

Rear Spring and Shock Absorber Replacement

Chock front wheels, jack rear of vehicle and place on blocks. Remove rear wheel. Jack up rear axle so that spring is slightly compressed. Loosen upper and lower spring attachments. Remove upper attachment for shock absorber. (Remove lower attachment also if removing shock absorber). Lower jack carefully and remove spring. Install new rear spring, taking previous steps in reverse order.

Steering Gear Assembly

The steering column of the 140 series has a break-away flange between the upper and lower steering column sections, which shears in the event of a frontal impact on the car. The 164 steering column has a break-away flange at the steering box which shears in the case of a frontal impact, and a sleeve in the column which collapses to absorb impact on the steering column.

Power Steering (164)

The optional 164 ZF power steering unit consists of a steering box, a pump, and a fluid reservoir. The power steering lowers the steering effort and reduces the number of turns of the steering wheel to 3.7 turns lock to lock.

Check the fluid level in the reservoir every 6000 miles. If it is lower than ¼ in. above the level mark, fill with automatic transmission oil, type A. Total capacity of the system is 2.5 pints (1.2 liters).

Since specialized testing equipment and tools are required for servicing the power steering unit, it is best to have a qualified Volvo service department do any repair work necessary.

Volvos employ several different types of steering systems which may be classified as either "cam or lever" or "cam and roller." The 144 employs the cam and roller type, while early production PV 444 and 445 employ the cam and lever types. Depending upon vehicle and steering gear model, the turning circle is about 33 feet. Ball joints not provided with grease fittings are plastic lined and require no lubrication.

Steering Wheel Replacement

Remove horn fuse. Remove screw from the top of the direction indicator switch housing and lift off the housing. Remove screw from top of steering wheel housing, lift up horn ring and remove. Remove steering wheel nut. Make sure direction indicator switch is in the neutral position, and with puller SVO 2711 (164, 140), SVO 2368 (PV 444/445), or SVO 2325 (PV 544, P 210) and the wheels pointed forward, remove steering wheel. When installing new steering wheel, tighten to torque of 23–35 ft. lbs. Replace horn fuse.

Steering Rod and Tie Rod Reconditioning

Bent or otherwise damaged steering rods and tie rods must be replaced, not straightened. Ball joints cannot be disassembled or adjusted, so they must also be replaced when worn or damaged. Steering rod ball joints are made with the rod, so the complete rod and ball joint assembly must be replaced. If the steering rod is to be removed, first remove the ball joint on the pitman arm and idler arm using the procedure described under "King Pin Replacement." Tie rod ball joints can be replaced individually and the same procedure can be used.

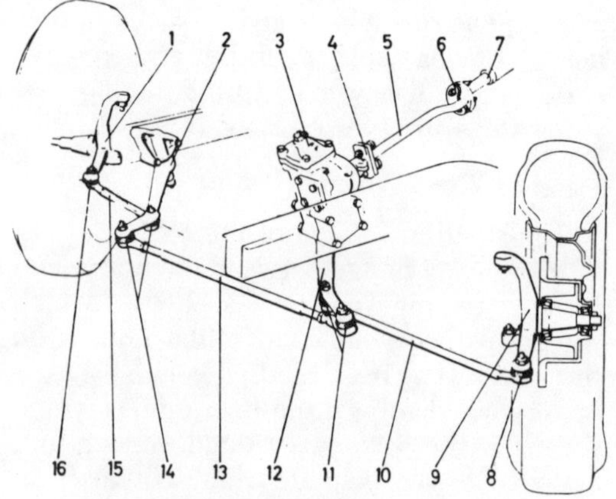

1. Steering knuckle
2. Relay arm
3. Steering gear housing
4. Lower steering column flange
5. Lower steering column section
6. Upper steering column flange
7. Upper steering column section
8. Ball joint
9. Steering knuckle
10. Steering rod
11. Ball joint
12. Pitman arm
13. Tie rod
14. Ball joint
15. Steering rod
16. Ball joint

Steering gear, 144.

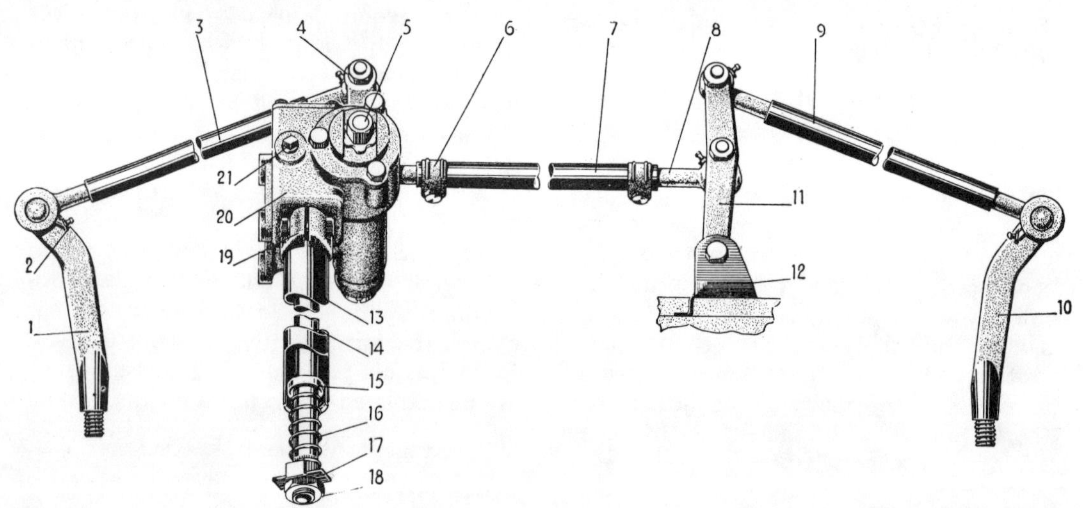

1. Left steering arm
2. Grease nipple
3. Left steering rod
4. Pitman arm
5. Adjusting screw
6. Clamp
7. Tie rod
8. Ball joint
9. Right steering rod
10. Right steering arm
11. Idler arm
12. Bracket for idler arm
13. Steering column housing
14. Steering column
15. Ball bearing
16. Spring
17. Locking washer
18. Nut
19. Clamp for housing
20. Steering gear housing
21. Grease plug

Steering gear, PV444, 445, 544, P210.

Chapter 10 Brakes

Description, Removal and Repair

Model P1800, 1800S and 122S have front wheel disc brakes and drum brakes at the rear, while the 144 and 142 have disc brakes on all four wheels. The PV 544 model employs drum brakes on all four wheels.

Disc Brakes

The disc type system consists of a brake disc which rotates with the wheel and a caliper having a hydraulic cylinder and piston on each side of the disc. The caliper presses friction pads against the disc to stop the car.

Brake Pad Inspection

Disc brake friction pads can be checked for wear using a gauge that measures the distance from the inside of one friction pad backing plate to the other when the brake is engaged. Brake pads should be replaced if worn down to a thickness of 1/16″.

Brake Pad Replacement

Jack up wheel and place vehicle on blocks. Remove wheel. Remove hairpin-shaped locking rings from guide pins. Pull out one of the lock pins while holding damper springs in place. Remove springs and other lock pin. Remove pads.

Carefully clean out cavity that holds pads. Replace any of the rubber covers that are damaged. If dirt has gotten into cylinder due to damaged cover, brake unit should be reconditioned. To make room for new brake pads, the plungers must be

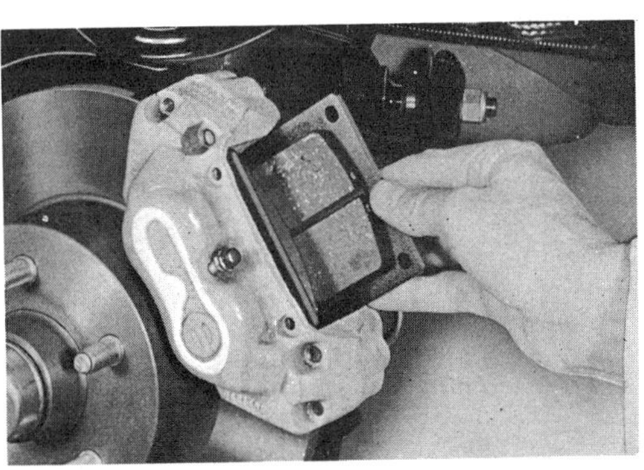

Removing disc brake pads.

pressed into the cylinders. This is facilitated by opening the air vent nipple. Close nipple after pressing in cylinders. Note also that the fluid in the master cylinder may rise and overflow when pressing in cylinders. Prevent fluid from getting on linings or brake disc. Install new pads and one of the lock pins, then damping springs and other lock pin. Install hairpin-shaped locking rings. Check that pads are movable. Press brake pedal several times to check that pedal is operating normally. As a rule bleeding is not required after replacing pads. Replace wheel and check brake fluid level in master cylinder.

Removing rear disc brake caliper.

Brake Caliper Replacement

Jack up vehicle and place on blocks. Remove wheel. Disconnect brake lines and tape openings to prevent dirt from entering and unnecessary leakage. Remove mounting bolts and brake caliper.

Place new caliper into position. See that contact surfaces are clean and not damaged, since the position of the caliper in relation to the brake disc is very important. Install mounting bolts and check to see that brake disc can rotate easily in the brake pads.

Checking disc brake runout.

Brake Disc Removal

The brake disc should be inspected for wear, run-out and thickness. Run-out must not exceed .004″ for the front wheel brakes and .006″ for the rear, at the outer edge of the disc. See first that wheel bearing adjustment is correct and that disc fits hub securely. Then use micrometer to check run-out of the brake disc. If brake disc is defective, it should be replaced. To do this, first remove brake caliper as described, then remove lock bolts and lift off brake disc. Tap on the inside of the disc several times with a plastic hammer.

Drum Brakes

Volvo drum brakes are of conventional design having the front and rear shoes pressed outward against an enclosing drum by a single, two-direction hydraulic cylinder. Equal braking is possible by having the wheel cylinders push the shoes out to initial drum contact with an extremely light pedal pressure. All shoes make contact evenly before full pressure is reached.

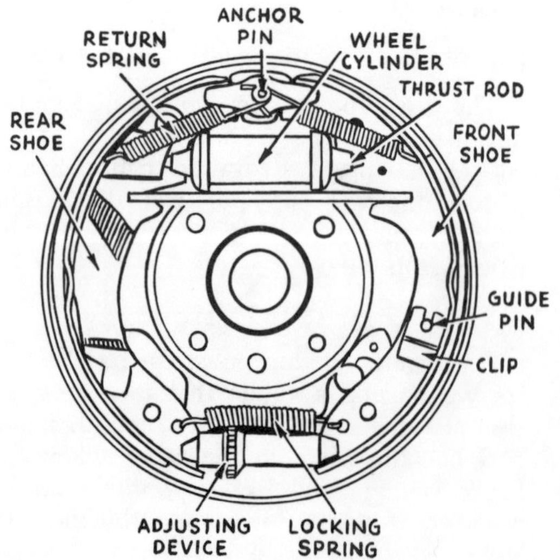

Right rear wheel brake drum.

Brake Shoe Replacement

Remove wheel and drum assembly for access to brake shoes. Disconnect locking spring, pull shoes apart and remove adjusting device. Remove locking clips at the sides.

Turn shoes outward until wheel cylinder thrust rods are released. Then turn shoes inward, release return springs and extract shoes for replacement or relining. If relining brake shoes, drill out lining rivets to avoid shoe rim distortion that punching-out causes. File off burrs around rivet holes. Keep hands clean while handling new linings.

Wheel Cylinder Inspection and Overhaul

Carefully pull lower edges of wheel cylinder boots away from cylinders and note if interior is wet—an indication of brake fluid seepage past the piston cup. If so, cylinder overhaul is required.

Clean dirt from all surrounding surfaces and then disconnect and seal off brake line (tape is often satisfactory for sealing). Remove cylinder from backing plate.

Dismantle boots, pistons, cups and spring from cylinder. Remove bleeder valve. Discard boots and cups; clean other parts with fresh brake fluid. Use no fluid containing even a trace of mineral oil.

Light scratches and corrosion can be polished from pistons and bore with fine emery cloth or steel wool. Dip all parts in brake fluid and reassemble. After installation, adjust brakes and road test for performance.

Brake Drum Inspection

Thoroughly clean and inspect brake drums for cracks, scoring and out-of-round. Polish out slight scores with emery cloth. Shallow grooves can be removed by boring provided oversized linings are obtainable. Out-of-round drums cause excessive wear on other brake parts as well as on tires. Maximum tolerable runout is .006″. Measure for run-out by checking along open and closed edges of machined surface and at right angles.

Before reinstalling brake drum, inspect all brake pipe and hose connections for fluid leakage. Tighten these connections and apply heavy pressure to brake pedal to recheck seal. Inspect rear wheel backing plate for leaks from wheel bearing oil seals. Replace seals if needed. Check all backing plate bolts for tightness. Clean away all dirt from assemblies and repack wheel bearings.

Master Cylinder

Series 140 Volvos utilize a dual master cylinder and two separate hydraulic circuits, one serving the right rear wheel and the lower set of two cylinders in each front wheel, and the other serving the left rear wheel and the upper set of cylinders in the front wheels. Thus, braking is still maintained even if one of the lines should fail.

Master Cylinder Overhaul

Disconnect and tape brake lines entering master cylinder. Remove mounting nuts and master cylinder, and pour out brake fluid. Hold master cylinder firmly in vise and with both hands lift fluid container up from rubber seals. Remove filler cap and strainer from container, as well as nuts and rubber seals from the cylinder. Remove brake contact and stop screw. Remove lock ring from primary plunger and remove plungers. If second plunger does not shake out, remove by blowing air in the hole for the brake contact.

1. Brake light contact
2. To left brake valve
3. To 6-branch union
4. Brake fluid container
5. To right brake valve
6. To 6-branch union
7. Master cylinder
8. Mounting bolt

Dual master brake cylinder.

Remove two seals from secondary plunger, being careful not to damage the surfaces of the plunger. If reconditioning, the primary plunger should be completely replaced, so it is not necessary to disassemble it. Clean all parts in fresh brake fluid and blow dry with compressed air. Then coat parts with brake fluid for reassembly. Examine cylinder carefully. If there are scores or scratches, cylinder should be replaced. If wear is suspected, measure diameter. Cylinder diameter should not exceed .881″, while plunger diameter should not be less than .870″. In addition to the primary plunger, the secondary plunger seals, the stop screw and washer, the circlip and the rubber seals for the fluid container should also be replaced.

Install plunger with seals and spring after dipping in brake fluid. Insert new primary plunger with washer and circlip. Check to see that hole for stop screw is clear and insert stop screw and sealing washer. Tighten to torque of 9.5 ft. lb. Check movement of plungers and make sure that through-flow holes are clear, including equalizer hole which can be checked with a soft copper, .5 mm diameter wire. If equalizer hole is not clear, master cylinder may be incorrectly assembled. Install container nuts with washers and rubber seals, container and brake contact.

Bleeding Brake System

Whenever any part of the hydraulic brake system has been removed, it is necessary to bleed air that has become trapped in the system. Also air can enter if quantity of fluid is too small, so first make sure the master cylinder is filled.

Connect one end of a bleeder hose to the air vent on the wheel brake unit and submerge the other end of the hose in a clean glass container partially filled with clean brake fluid. While a helper depresses the brake pedal, open the air nipple, and repeat until the brake fluid that flows out is free of air bubbles. Bleed in this order for 140 Series cars: left rear, right front upper nipple, left front upper nipple, right rear, right front inside and outside lower nipples, left front inside and outside lower nipples. Frequently check

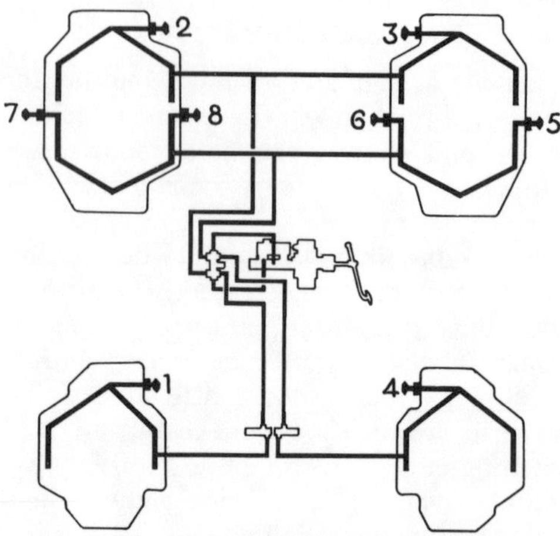

1. Left rear wheel valve
2. Left front wheel upper inner valve
3. Right front wheel, upper inner valve
4. Right rear wheel valve
5. Right front wheel, outer valve
6. Right front wheel, lower inner valve
7. Left front wheel, outer valve
8. Left front wheel, lower inner valve

Hydraulic brake bleeding sequence, series 140 and 164.

Bleeding left rear brake unit.

level of fluid in master cylinder and fill if low. Do not use fluid bled from system.

Brake Booster

The brake booster available on 140 Series Volvos reduces required foot pressure for braking approximately 25%. The booster is mechanically controlled by the foot pedal and conveys this pressure along with an engine vacuum assistance to the dual master cylinder. A vacuum control valve prevents air from flowing back into booster when engine is not running. The valve must be replaced when defective.

Checking Brake Booster Operation

The operation of the brake booster can be checked easily. With engine off, use up all vacuum by depressing brake pedal several times. Hold pedal down and start engine. As vacuum builds, the pedal will move farther (held under same foot pressure) as power is developed by booster. Check out the booster vacuum system along the hose, at the vacuum valve, and at all connections. Inspect filter for restriction. If the booster is defective, it must be replaced.

Brake Booster Replacement

Remove master cylinder. Disconnect fork at front of booster from brake pedal and disconnect vacuum hose from check valve. Remove four mounting screws from bracket and lift booster cylinder forward.

Loosen lock nut and unscrew fork. Remove rubber cover and thrust rod from cylinder. Assemble in reverse order of above, and bleed the entire brake system.

Brake Specifications

	Type		*Brake Cyl. Bore (In.)*			*Drum or Disc Diam. (In.)*	
			Master Cyl.	*Wheel Cyl.*			
Model	*Front*	*Rear*		*Front*	*Rear*	*Front*	*Rear*
PV444	Drum	Drum					
PV544	Drum	Drum	1	1	.813	9	9
122, P1800	Disc	Drum					
142, 144	Disc	Disc	.882	1.422	1.422	10.7	11.6
145	Disc	Disc	.882	1.422	1.5	10.7	11.6
164	Disc	Disc	.95	1.422	1.422	10.7	11.6

New brake lining thickness is .394 in.

Conversion—Metric and U.S. Measures

Linear Units (Distance, Length, Angle)

1 kilometer = 0.6214 miles or 3,280 feet
1 mile = 1.6093 kilometers
Multiply kilometers by 0.6214 to get miles. Multiply miles by 1.6093 to get kilometers.
1 kilometer = 1000 meters
1 meter = 3.281 feet or 39.370 inches
1 centimeter = 0.394 inches
1 inch = 2.540 centimeters
Multiply centimeters by 0.394 to get inches. Multiply inches by 2.54 to get centimeters.

Cubic Units (Volume, Displacement)

1 liter = 1000 cubic centimeters
1 cubic centimeter (milliliter) = 0.061 cubic inches
1 cubic inch = 16.387 cubic centimeters
Multiply cubic centimeters by 0.61 to get cubic inches. Multiply cubic inches by 16.387 to get cubic centimeters.
1 liter = 0.264 gallons = 1.057 quarts = 2.1 pints
1 gallon = 3.785 liters = 231 cubic inches
Multiply liters by 0.264 to get gallons. Multiply gallons by 231 to get cubic inches.

Engine displacement—Cubic inch displacement is found by multiplying the bore by itself; multiplying this answer by 0.7854; multiplying this answer by the stroke; and multiplying this answer by the number of cylinders.

The constant 0.7854 is used rather than π (the mathematical constant, 3.14159) because the bore of the cylinder is the diameter. not the radius.

Using π, the formula is:

$$\left(\frac{\text{bore}}{2}\right)^2 \text{ x } \pi \text{ x (stroke) x (\# cylinders)}$$
$$= \text{displacement}$$

The same formula is used to determine the displacement of an engine in metric units (centimeters), but only after the millimeter bore and stroke dimensions are changed to centimeters. Change millimeters to centimeters by dividing by ten.

Force Units (Pressure, Torque)

1 atmosphere (atm) = 14.7 pounds per sq. in. (psi)
1 psi = 0.68 atmosphere
Pressure is measured as force against a surface, not volume. A bicycle tire at 50 psi has far less air in it than a car tire having 17 psi.
1 kilogram per sq. centimeter = 14.223 lbs. sq. in.
1 kilogram-meter = 7.233 foot-lbs.
A foot-pound is a unit of force equal to one pound raised one foot. An inch-pound is one pound raised one inch.

BRITISH IMPERIAL AND U.S. LIQUID MEASURES

	Imperial	*U.S.*
gallon	277.4 (cu. in.)	231 (cu. in.)
quart	69.4	57.8
pint	34.7	28.9

GASOLINE CONSUMPTION (by miles and kilometers)

1 mile per gallon = 0.355 kilometers per liter
30 miles per gallon = 10.64 kilometers per liter
1 kilometer per liter = 2.82 miles per gallon
8 kilometers per liter = 22.6 miles per gallon

COMMON AUTOMOTIVE ABBREVIATIONS

L	=	liters
mm	=	millimeters
ohv	=	overhead valves
CIH	=	camshaft in cylinder head (rocker arm required)
ohc	=	overhead camshaft (no rocker arm required)
bhp	=	braking horsepower
SAE	=	Society of Automotive Engineers
rpm	=	revolutions per minute
ft.-lbs.	=	foot-pounds (unit of force)
in.-lbs.	=	inch-pounds
POE	=	port of entry

Conversion—Millimeters to Decimal Inches

mm	*inches*	*mm*	*inches*	*mm*	*inches*	*mm*	*inches*	*mm*	*inches*
1	.039 370	31	1.220 470	61	2.401 570	91	3.582 670	210	8.267 700
2	.078 740	32	1.259 840	62	2.440 940	92	3.622 040	220	8.661 400
3	.118 110	33	1.299 210	63	2.480 310	93	3.661 410	230	9.055 100
4	.157 480	34	1.338 580	64	2.519 680	94	3.700 780	240	9.448 800
5	.196 850	35	1.377 949	65	2.559 050	95	3.740 150	250	9.842 500
6	.236 220	36	1.417 319	66	2.598 420	96	3.779 520	260	10.236 200
7	.275 590	37	1.456 689	67	2.637 790	97	3.818 890	270	10.629 900
8	.314 960	38	1.496 050	68	2.677 160	98	3.858 260	280	11.032 600
9	.354 330	39	1.535 430	69	2.716 530	99	3.897 630	290	11.417 300
10	.393 700	40	1.574 800	70	2.755 900	100	3.937 000	300	11.811 000
11	.433 070	41	1.614 170	71	2.795 270	105	4.133 848	310	12.204 700
12	.472 440	42	1.653 540	72	2.834 640	110	4.330 700	320	12.598 400
13	.511 810	43	1.692 910	73	2.874 010	115	4.527 550	330	12.992 100
14	.551 180	44	1.732 280	74	2.913 380	120	4.724 400	340	13.385 800
15	.590 550	45	1.771 650	75	2.952 750	125	4.921 250	350	13.779 500
16	.629 920	46	1.811 020	76	2.992 120	130	5.118 100	360	14.173 200
17	.669 290	47	1.850 390	77	3.031 490	135	5.314 950	370	14.566 900
18	.708 660	48	1.889 760	78	3.070 860	140	5.511 800	380	14.960 600
19	.748 030	49	1.929 130	79	3.110 230	145	5.708 650	390	15.354 300
20	.787 400	50	1.968 500	80	3.149 600	150	5.905 500	400	15.748 000
21	.826 770	51	2.007 870	81	3.188 970	155	6.102 350	500	19.685 000
22	.866 140	52	2.047 240	82	3.228 340	160	6.299 200	600	23.622 000
23	.905 510	53	2.086 610	83	3.267 710	165	6.496 050	700	27.559 000
24	.944 880	54	2.125 980	84	3.307 080	170	6.692 900	800	31.496 000
25	.984 250	55	2.165 350	85	3.346 450	175	6.889 750	900	35.433 000
26	1.023 620	56	2.204 720	86	3.385 820	180	7.086 600	1000	39.370 000
27	1.062 990	57	2.244 090	87	3.425 190	185	7.283 450	2000	78.740 000
28	1.102 360	58	2.283 460	88	3.464 560	190	7.480 300	3000	118.110 000
29	1.141 730	59	2.322 830	89	3.503 903	195	7.677 150	4000	157.480 000
30	1.181 100	60	2.362 200	90	3.543 300	200	7.874 000	5000	196.850 000

To change decimal millimeters to decimal inches, position the decimal point where desired on either side of the millimeter measurement shown and reset the inches decimal by the same number of digits in the same direction. For example, to convert .001 mm into decimal inches, reset the decimal behind the 1 mm (shown on the chart) to .001; change the decimal inch equivalent (.039″ shown) to .00039″).

Conversion—Common Fractions to Decimals and Millimeters

Common Fractions	*Decimal Fractions*	*Millimeters (approx.)*	*Common Fractions*	*Decimal Fractions*	*Millimeters (approx.)*	*Common Fractions*	*Decimal Fractions*	*Millimeters (approx.)*
1/128	.008	0.20	11/32	.344	8.73	43/64	.672	17.07
1/64	.016	0.40	23/64	.359	9.13	11/16	.688	17.46
1/32	.031	0.79	3/8	.375	9.53	45/64	.703	17.86
3/64	.047	1.19	25/64	.391	9.92	23/32	.719	18.26
1/16	.063	1.59	13/32	.406	10.32	47/64	.734	18.65
5/64	.078	1.98	27/64	.422	10.72	3/4	.750	19.05
3/32	.094	2.38	7/16	.438	11.11	49/64	.766	19.45
7/64	.109	2.78	29/64	.453	11.51	25/32	.781	19.84
1/8	.125	3.18	15/32	.469	11.91	51/64	.797	20.24
9/64	.141	3.57	31/64	.484	12.30	13/16	.813	20.64
5/32	.156	3.97	1/2	.500	12.70	53/64	.828	21.03
11/64	.172	4.37	33/64	.516	13.10	27/32	.844	21.43
3/16	.188	4.76	17/32	.531	13.49	55/64	.859	21.83
13/64	.203	5.16	35/64	.547	13.89	7/8	.875	22.23
7/32	.219	5.56	9/16	.563	14.29	57/64	.891	22.62
15/64	.234	5.95	37/64	.578	14.68	29/32	.906	23.02
1/4	.250	6.35	19/32	.594	15.08	59/64	.922	23.42
17/64	.266	6.75	39/64	.609	15.48	15/16	.938	23.81
9/32	.281	7.14	5/8	.625	15.88	61/64	.953	24.21
19/64	.297	7.54	41/64	.641	16.27	31/32	.969	24.61
5/16	.313	7.94	21/32	.656	16.67	63/64	.984	25.00
21/64	.328	8.33						

Automotive Parts Terminology

In some cases there is more than one name for an automobile part or assembly. Equivalent meanings are given below. "Br" stands for British.

Carburetor

air correction jet (Br), high speed air bleed
butterfly, throttle valve, throttle plate
choke tube (Br), venturi
emulsion tube (Br), main vent tube
idle speed screw, throttle stop screw
main jet (Br), main metering jet
pilot jet (Br), idling jet
pilot jet air bleed (Br), idle air adjusting screw
progression circuit (Br), second idle stage
slow-running adjustment (Br), idle speed adjustment
slow-running volume adjustment (Br), idle mixture adjustment
strangler (Br), choke

Engine

bearing insert, bearing shell, bearing
core plug (Br), welsh plug, drain plug
crankpin, journal
gudgeon pin (Br), piston pin, wrist pin
retaining clip, circlip, snapring
scraper ring, oil ring
clutch driven plate, drive disc
oil sump, oil pan
slave cylinder, servo cylinder, operating cylinder

Electrical

alternator, AC generator
dynamo, generator
earth, ground
distributor shaft, driving spindle

Suspension

king pin slant, steering knuckle inclination, swivel axle
control arm, control link, wishbone
cross member, assembly member

Miscellaneous

filling up, topping up
bushings, bushes, shell bearings
fork, yoke
brake backing plate, securing plate
spanner, wrench

Miscellaneous Specifications

Specification	*B-16*	*B-18*	*B-20*	*B-30*
Maximum Flywheel runout (in) @ diam. (in.)	.008	.002 @ 5.90	.002 @ 5.90	.002 @ 5.90
Camshaft Bearing Clear. (in.)	.0010-.0029	.0008-.0030	.0008-.0030	.0008-.0030
Camshaft end-play (in.)	–	.0008-.0024	.0008-.0024	.0008-.0024
Timing gear backlash (in)	.0004-.0016	.0016-.0032	.0016-.0032	.0016-.0032
Timing gear tooth flank clear. (in.)	–	.0016-.0032	–	–
Oil Pump Gear end-play (in)	.0008-.0040	.0008-.0040	.0008-.0040	.0008-.0040
Oil Pump Gear Back-lash (in.)	.006-.014	.006-.014	.006-.014	.006-.014
Oil Press. Relief spring free lgth. (in)	1.22	1.22	1.54	1.54
Rear Axle Ratio	–	4.10:1 or 4.56:1	4.10:1 or 4.30:1	3.31:1 or 3.73:1
Rear Axle Gear Back-lash (in.)	–	.004-.008	.004-.008	.005-.008
Rear Axle ① Pinion Preload (in/lb)	–	9.55-20	9.55-20	9.55-20
Differential Bearing Preload (in.)	–	.005-.008	.005-.008	.005-.008

① New bearings.